USED:

NOT A MEMOIR

SLOANE ELLIS

For Dad

INTRODUCTION

Life is a grindstone. Whether it grinds you down, or polishes you up depends on the stuff he's made of.

-John Billings

Anachronist

Summer 2010.

I am traversing the passenger door of a rapidly accelerating entry-level BMW, Audi, Benz, or some other douchebag, wannabe wagon with tan guts. My only tether to life is the bloody popped collar of a man I do not know. Just over nine years ago, I entered my first rehabilitation center for drug addiction, not knowing at the time the soul-searching, and soul-crushing, journey I was beginning. Right now, what I do know is that my bare feet have lost pace with the car as it swerves back and forth and now drag on the freshly paved macadam. Five years ago, I watched my father choke to death on his own blood, a tragic end to a life blighted by alcoholism. Five years from now, I would add another stamp to my rehab passport, exploring the hope and horror of a twenty-eight-day inpatient booking, wondering how I possibly could have gotten this bad. Just twelve hours ago, I was smiling at how good my life was, drinking my first beer of the day, poured from a tap tower installed in my very own home bar; it was my pride and joy and the last thing an alcoholic and drug addict should have at his disposal. Twelve hours from now, I am lying to my wife about why the top of my foot is missing. Turns out, when apparent death is imminent, it's not just the greatest hits of your life shuffling through the writhing neurons in your brain, but also things that haven't happened yet. My sudden powers of prophecy are less divination and more self-fulfillment.

Confused yet? It gets worse.

Back to my imminent death by possible vehicular manslaughter and my own stupidity, I rely on action movie physics and try to climb through the open window. Six hours ago, I had my first meal of the day, after about twelve standard alcoholic drinks. It was not enough to soak up the deluge of insanity that would ensue. Three hours ago, I do not remember because I later realized I was in an alcoholic blackout. I surmised this because friends I spoke with in the coming days would say they saw me during this time and claimed I appeared completely lucid. I was always a happy drunk, until I was not. One hour ago, there is also a gap in my memory, but as the story goes, related by friends and family present on the scene, in the basement of an urban-chic pub in a provincial Philadelphia suburb, someone, likely the dude I am now hanging from, said something that made me "turn green," invoking the color and temperament of the Incredible Hulk, a favorite comic character and fictional persona I would come to embody more than once in my life. A fight ensued, we all were tossed out, and when the "bad guys'" ride arrived, one of them could not resist getting the last word in as they drove off.

Back to my dragging feet, I feel searing pain along my arches, my right foot being degloved by the macadam conveyor belt sliding along beneath, but it is far away, happening to someone else. "Degloving" enjoys a more macabre place in the lexicon of medical terminology, and typically refers to the skin and then fascia, the layer you only see after your brown or bronze or golden-brown or olive or yellow or freckled or albino complexion is being torn from its origin point by a shearing force, in most cases, a limb. Imagine peeling the sheath from a banana, exposing its meaty fruit. The same thing was happening to my foot, turning it into a meat crayon, drawing a bloody line with a toddler's artistic force across the solid yellow ones on the street. I remember this part of the night because of the exquisite pain. As an active drug addict and alcoholic, it is impossible to keep pace with time. Pain is about the only thing in the last twenty years that forced my focus on the present, rather than regretting the past or racing ahead, always restless, irritable, and discontent with who I was, always asking the universe, "Is this it?"

Eight years from now, I would execute what my ex-wife, the love of my life, that death of one days after the other kind of love, calls an "extraordinary betrayal," forever altering her life and the lives of our two children, eventually landing in my third attempt at rehabilitation. At present, with stark clarity, I recall trying to claw and climb into the window, but the bloody shirt collar, my lanyard to life, tears free. I claw my hand up to this mystery man's face, fish-hooking my fingers into his mouth for a new anchor. As any rational person being assaulted by an untreated addict with psychopathic tendencies would, he bites hard. More pain, more memory.

Nine years ago, in love and in awe, months after admitting but not accepting I was a drug addict, I married the only woman that could have saved me from myself, making a desperate promise, implied within the vows of "in sickness and health," that I would stay sober. Nine years from now, amid the din of a flickering "Auto Tags" sign, C.C., the girl I dreamed of since the day I realized life meant finding the person that would help you live it, fighting the staccato sharp inhales and exhales of a silent sob, signed our divorce decree. After she was done, the notary, having witnessed this scene too many times, slid the document over to me.

Even with the analgesic properties of alcohol poisoning, the mumbling survival instinct in my pickled brain says it is time to let go. My hands make that blunted squeaking sound as they slide down the car door and I hit the road, the rear passenger GT radial rolling over my left leg and arm with a "bump, bump." The jerkoffs in the car bounce twice, then escape off the bypass. Criminals on the run. Criminal on the ground. Nine years from now, I am on a rush-hour raceway after speaking with a narcotics agent who wants to put me in prison, and for few pounds of my heart, I take my hand off the wheel. Bump, bump. Bump, bump. Bump, bump.

Hi. I am an alcoholic, drug addict, narcissist, self-centered egoist, pathological liar, occasional nihilist, with borderline histrionic and personality disorder and a dusting of sociopathy and psychopathy, but the only real problem I ever had was a person called Sloane; that is me. If you have ever been to an Alcoholics Anonymous (AA) meeting, you may recognize this riff on the standard introduction of oneself before speaking, where you say who you are followed by your problem. So, who am I? I am just an average man—average height, average intelligence, average, well — you know. I am not a Hollywood hunk or sports legend or platinum YouTube darling. I never considered myself a pioneer, but I was responsible for the restructuring of the illegal drug and impaired practitioner policy at three different medical institutions. Perhaps the greatest things I have done were all the ones I have done wrong. I am no one special; I used to think I was and that was the root of all my problems. You could walk by me on the street and never notice me. I could be anyone, because wherever I was, I tried to blend in, switching out my memes and masks for the appropriate occasion, or I could be no one, retreating from the harsh light of the real as I have for most of my life, or I could be the guy who saves your life.

This is not a memoir about addiction—there are already many stellar texts on the topic that I could not hope to expand upon—but as my struggles with it laid the foundation for the person I am today, much of my tale is framed through the lens of that devastating disease. And I believe it is a disease, be it social, moral, spiritual, or physical—not just because of my background as a registered nurse but because it lies dormant not only in our genes, but it is also woven into our cultures and history. We are all addicted to something, be it booze or drugs, even other people or ideas, but society says you are only an addict if you get caught. I once knew a man who admitted he was addicted to love, and if you can believe someone can get hooked on such a nebulous mud of emotion and neurotransmitters, it is not hard to understand why we get addicted to the predictable euphoria of opiates and cocaine or socially acceptable vices like alcohol, nicotine, and social media. Everybody's got their something.

But what many of us fail to realize is that addiction to a person, place, thing, or pattern is not our problem; it is a solution to the real problem—us. That is why I list all my sins and the labels I have collected through my life first, followed by my name; I was the only thing wrong with me. Most of my adult life has been hours of self-seeking smeared out among decades of playing at being a functional human being. For more than twenty years, I have consistently plied at one thing: numbing myself to the loss of a life I never tried to live, while wasting the beautiful one I was pretending to.

I do not know what it feels like to be a "normie." You know, the idealized versions of people in commercials, absurdly happy while sipping Starbucks and eating avocado toast, going out for "a drink" after work, or regaling in your relevance through Instagram reels. I do not feel the urge to stock up on milk and eggs at the site of a snowflake or trample others on my way to a new game console on Black Friday. I do not care about politics or religion or feel the need to spew my personal thoughts on Facebook for all to stamp happy, sad, angry, or poop emoticons beneath. I put "normie" in quotes because you can refer to yourself as "we" now and no one is supposed to bat an eye. There is no established norm anymore. Nor should there be. Ostensibly, you can be whoever or whatever you want to be. Unless you are an addict —then you cannot be that. Now you are "sober curious." There are no commercials of us, our eyes rolling back into our head after emptying a syringe full of heroin in our arm, while friends burst with rapturous laughter; no quick ads before a selected YouTube video of us stumbling out of a bar and fumbling with keys before getting into a car. There is only a quick cable access channel PSA asking if you or a loved one suffers from addiction. We think differently and that is not inherently by choice. Unless you have struggled with addiction, you have no idea what it feels like to have your body jerked along with puppet strings, your mind overridden with irrational thoughts that make perfect sense to you. We don't care about cancel culture, only our culture of consequence. The fallout of our actions while using our respective vices, regardless of intent, affects much more than us. The people who care about us most—our spouses, our children, our families and friends—take the full force of our shock wave. But this is not an autobiography of a man who gave up everything for just one thing, nor is it an account of love and loss and the refusal to see what is right in front of you until it is too late.

Fifteen years ago, I watched my father die. While most fathers teach their sons how to become men, I took away a very different lesson from mine as I watched frothy red foam rise from my dying dad's mouth. I made an oath to myself that day that I would not share the same fate. For as long as I knew him, my father was an alcoholic. I first heard that term long before I truly understood what it meant and even longer before I fully appreciated the

my grandparents, on Princeton Avenue, named, I imagi
only other prestigious Ivy League school within drivin
besides the University of Pennsylvania, Princeton University.
Even then, it was not an area that could be considered on par
with the provincial Princeton, New Jersey; it was a blue-collar
town, filled with hardworking people, its streets dotted with local
businesses. It was a nice place to live. My grandfather, the OG
Thomas William Ellis, was one of the finest men I have ever
known. He served in the military during World War II and
returned home to Philly to work at the dockyard until his retirement. He was a humble and modest man who lived for his family.
With his tall stature and barrel chest he reminded me of the oak
trees that lined the street of our first home on Fuller Street, where
we moved when I was five.

My grandmother, had she been around when YouTube
became a thing, could have become an indie-darling with her
show, *Cooking with Butter*. She was from Shenandoah Valley, an
ultramarathon north of Philly. It is likely her DNA became
steeped with all things calorically rich from all the neighboring
Amish farms in her backyard. To this day, I have never been able
to replicate her pancakes, with their crisp edges and sour cream
donut texture. A couple more pats of butter on top and drench
them in syrup and that was why I was a fat little kid. Then there
were the mountains of made-from-scratch Christmas cookies,
butter cake from Stocks Bakery (yep, that is a thing), Tastykakes,
hoagies (no such thing as a sub in or around Philly), and the only
real soft pretzel. Every kid eats shit, unless you are one of those
annoying parents that blended up your own baby food and baked
muffins full of carrots and cauliflower, and many avoid childhood
diabetes and obesity, but I do not bring up these visions of satu-
rated fat dancing in my head out of pure nostalgia; the obsessive-
ness with which I looked forward to these treats, in retrospect,
may have been the embryo of addiction, beginning its division

and multiplication. Or it was just the easiest way to keep me quiet. Apparently, I was one of those asshole toddlers no one wanted to babysit.

Being a little fat kid, even though the tags on my clothes called me husky, was a great way to jump-start a life of shame. I recall tearful conversations with my mom asking to change schools and find new friends. Running away and burying my head in junk food was the only coping mechanism I had. I envied friends who now recall their childhood as a wide-open vista, full of laughter and nostalgia. I remember mine as warped images thumbed through a view master, the slides smudged and marred with crayon. Even then, I was an "anachronist," the boy out of time, a term I adopted from some science fiction novel I read in school, always feeling I had been placed there, never wanting to be where I was. None of us have a choice where we start, but most of us eventually find our way forward. I never felt like my life ran along a clear line; I always veered off a path I was on and struggled to get back. I marvel at my children who, today at the ages of eighteen and fifteen, have more ironclad ideas of who they are and what they want to do with their lives than I ever did. For a long time, I felt I could never know myself until I was backed into a corner, when desperation takes over and I claw my way forward, finding a tentative peace of mind until it all starts over again. I relied too heavily on people telling me who I should be—first my mom, later my wife, and all the real people in between.

I did not come from money, but me and my siblings never wanted for anything. Sure, we wanted things we could not get, and sometimes ate pancakes for dinner (Mom's boring Bisquick, not Grandma's bangers), but we had presents under the Christmas tree every year, vacations every summer, even went to Disney World twice; we had a decent upbringing. My mother was a homemaker, until she was no longer able to be. She raised the four of us practically on her own. She lived for her "babies," as my father used to say. She really did. My dad was not around much, and she often played both roles in our home. She was the cook, maid, tutor, coach, mentor, life coach, disciplinarian, whip-cracker (it was a belt, or shoe), chauffeur, and just about anything a child, or adult, needed. "Saint Peg," as she was colloquially known among the "gang," our extended host of blood relatives and friends. She is God-fearing, devoted to her family and altruistic to a fault. She is tough, one of the toughest people I know. She suffered from a rare heart condition where roughly every seven years, her heart rate would race above 200 beats per minute (BPM) while standing still; a normal resting heart rate is typically between 60 and 100 BPM. This happened to her once when I was bout sixteen and she had just dropped me off at my summer job as a lifeguard. On the drive home, she felt her heart racing and her vision dimming; when your heart is pumping that fast, blood tends to pool up inside it instead of getting shuttled to vital organs, like your brain. Most people would pull over and, back then, find a pay phone to call 911; but not her. She drove another three miles to an emergency room and explained the situation. Medical technology had advanced since her last episode and a cardiologist was able to ablate, or burn out, the aberrant electrical signal in her heart. She never gave up on anything or anyone, least of all me, but I put her through her paces.

I lived in a modest duplex, essentially a full house with a plaster wall spread right down the middle, splitting it into two chiral halves with my mom, dad, and three younger siblings. I had a good childhood, all things considered. We lived in a neighborhood where you grew up with the same people, for better or worse. It seemed simpler then. I realize that now as a father, in an affluent suburb of Philadelphia, where I have watched my two children cycle through the amount of people I would have called "friend" during my entire life in less than half that time. I was an Irish Catholic kid and went to Catholic school—all of us pasty white save for the sole African American boy I shared classes with for twelve years. There were eight years of elementary education, four years of high school (I'm still trying to figure out the whole middle school thing), and then you got out; either you went to college, the military, or became a "Nasty Neastie"—that is, you stayed. I am not putting down my fellow countrymen and - women. I even moved back to the house I was raised in for a few years after college graduation with a real job and everything; that would not be the last time I sought refuge in my childhood home. There is just this effect that lifers in my old neighborhood would contract, jumping from one shit job to the next for years with no endgame in mind; most of their nights would end in a dive bar along Frankford Avenue, the main drag through NE Philly, rarely able to afford spending a night down in the city from which they are proud to say they hail.

They were not all sob stories. Some friends I have that remained found love, started families and jobs they enjoy, and are content with their lives. I even have family friends that are regular local celebrities, owning a chain of bars and enjoying great success in both center city Philadelphia and the "Neast." Of course, I would not trust most of them to watch my house while I was away. And much of my family still lives there and seems happy. So, while there is nothing inherently wrong with the neighborhoods besides the endless cycle of filtering and gentrification, spending my entire life there just was not what I wanted. So, I got out. Or, rather, I found someone who got me out—the ex–Love of my Life, C.C.. Without her, it is highly likely that, not only would I have not left my hometown, but I would also not have been one of the, albeit subjective, success stories cemented among the brick, mortar, and legends of the avenues and boulevards either.

We lived that blue-collar life that often ran roughshod over what we wanted, caught up in the whirlwind of getting four kids safely carted to school or work or the market or staying at Grandmom's or an aunt's house. School was out and my father was saddled with an impromptu "take your kid to work" day. Dad's old truck lost its shocks long ago and the ride from Philly to the landfill of New Jersey was a bumpy one. I looked forward to the paved potential of the upcoming bridge, but I was getting sleepy and slumped against the passenger door. I could hear a rattle inside it, which, to my young ears, did not sound like anything amiss. This is the part in the family drama thriller where we crosscut to the inside of the car door, tight on the components of the lock, blown up and shifting unnaturally. Cut back to me snoozing against the door, my long eyelashes draped over my cheekbones, oblivious to the chaos inside my pillow. Cut to my dad, the same resigned look on his face as he takes the same ride he has for years. Back to the jiggling lock parts that should be still, the rattling getting louder, absorbing the bumps in the road. Cut to the worn tires of Dad's truck going *bump, bump* as we roll onto the smooth sailing off the bridge. The rattling lock is silent. I am still snoozing, missing my big moment. Then the door falls open and my eyes snap open to see that smooth pavement of the bridge sliding by. Before I have a chance for any of my short life to flash before me, my dad yanks me back so hard, I fly into the other door, which stays closed. I am in his lap, we are still driving, and my dad says, "You're okay, buddy." With my dad, there were no questions; things just were. My dad was my hero, even years later, when I could barely stand to look at him or speak to him.

My father was a walking tragedy. He was an alcoholic and it killed him piece by piece. I never heard the word *alcoholic* or comprehended what it meant until I was old enough to be an altar boy, lectured to by old men on the sin of masturbation as I dressed them for Mass. I know what you are thinking. C.C. thought the same thing decades later when she struggled to put my inability to stay sober into perspective. In desperation, right where I drove her, scraping my past for any possible explanation for fucking up our life yet again, she looked at me dead-faced and asked me if I could have possibly been molested by a priest during my tenure as an altar boy, the moldy memory bricked up in my subconscious, floating out spores that eroded my sanity and self-control. That did not happen, at least I am pretty sure it did not, but that was the fallout of this disease, the people we care about most catching the shrapnel of our choices and actions, just as me, my mom, and my siblings did from my dad.

My father was always "Fun Daddy." When he was home, he was always laughing and horsing around with me and my siblings, with a drawl perpetually slurred by Budweiser. He was less the dad that read you bedtime stories and more the one who drops you on your head (that only happened once and Vinny was fine), but he was a good man. He often went out of his way to help family and friends, offering pro bono plumbing work. He once traveled to Ireland solely to install a shower in a stone hut for a friend. Nestled in one the Emerald Isle's ubiquitous green fields, there was barely enough water pressure to manage a trickle from the shower head. Still, he tried. And the promise of being immersed in a culture steeped in Jameson and Guinness was too enticing to pass up. He probably still just drank Bud. He was a good man, right up to the point where he died too soon.

As the breadwinner in the family, he was not around much throughout our childhood. Most of our interaction with him was late at night when we would sneak down to share pizza with him after he got home from work. Other "take your kid to work days" with my dad consisted of driving through Philly from job to job, watching him shew prostitutes away from his truck, adding to my colorful vocabulary of swear words, and occasionally learning how to solder pipes and diagnose leaks. The man was a piece of iron. He would walk through the door to our home at night with injuries that would have made an emergency room nurse nauseous; he would just soak his mangled limbs in Betadine and crack open a beer. But it was an extended stay in a hospital that first exposed his physical dependence on alcohol.

As an anesthetist, one of the first questions I ask patients I am about to put under anesthesia is if they consume alcohol, and if so, how much. This is not to shame anyone; I need to know for their own safety and mine. Recovering after knee surgery, his body bereft of alcohol for a few days, my dad had a grand mal seizure. Like all things, except addicts, our bodies crave balance. When we upset that balance, our bodies show a remarkable ability to adapt, until they cannot. Alcohol blunts our inhibitions, cures social anxiety, and wakes us up in strange bedrooms, but it also blunts our natural excitatory pathways and ability to remain conscious. The more we drink, the more our body amps up those neural connections so we do not pass out. If we stop suddenly, as my dad did, all that innate adrenaline counteracting the alcohol now courses through our brain unabated. Once we cross the seizure threshold, our bodies convulse and contort and can potentially die. This can happen anywhere at any time; fortunately for my father, he was in a hospital. It is likely even my dad did not know how much he was drinking each day, let alone my mother, so the medical staff was in the dark about the possibility of this happening. We are often our own worst enemies, and rarely do we admit to things of which we are not proud. As a result, if someone does admit how much they drink in an interview, I assume it is double that amount.

Some hide their drinking; we hid an alcoholic. Like all the horrors in our family, we did our best to cover it up. There were no discussions about why Dad kept falling down the stairs, no debriefs when he got pulled over with me and my younger siblings in the car, completely trashed. When Dad became too sick to work and support us, my mother picked up the pieces and went to work full-time. It was how she dealt with it all, and with her constant encouragement and pushing for me and my siblings to succeed and move on, it was how she taught us to deal with it too. He was still with us, but we already talked about him in the past tense remembering the good and the bad. I loved his laugh

—a de-crescendoing baritone that sounded like pure joy, or at least genuine amusement. I loved how he would show me he was still awake while he lay with me when I was too scared to sleep. I watched him work, I watched him kiss my mother as she hugged him with love. I watched him roll down the stairs to the basement to get more beer after he and my mom had a fight, and she would storm out. I would wait like a dog watching its owner leave, thinking they would never return, but she always did, with bags full of groceries. Years later, on the rare occasion I would go into a grocery store in the late evening, anytime I saw a woman shopping on her own, I wondered if she was contemplating going back with groceries or leaving for good.

What I remember most about being a kid was fear. I believe everything we do is fear-based. Fear-based thought and action is a mantra in sobriety literature. It sounds ambiguous and facile, but fear is likely the oldest, most primal emotion experienced by all living things. Our primordial brain, or lizard brain, is mostly governed by fear, evoking a "fight or flight" response under severe stress. Addiction taps into these primal responses, hijacking our base instincts, once governed by hunger or pain or lust, to seek out our vice with terrifying conviction. It is insanity in its purest form.

I went to elementary school back when they still showed that terrifying animated video of getting a rabies shot. Relative to the vapid computer-generated techniques used in most animation today, this cautionary tale was beautifully hand-drawn, using the analogy of soldiers marching out of the ten syringes that were injected into your abdomen to fight the quickly fatal disease. I do not know if this video still exists but consider yourself lucky if you are young enough to have avoided it. Decades of parent groups and lawsuits have cooled most of the fire and brimstone of Catholic school, but back then, nuns were scary. I was not a stellar student, academically, but I never felt the dread of being held back a grade. After blossoming from a problematic toddler

He is a good man, another blue-collar champ and, as an iron worker, as hard as the rivets he slammed through steel. As I was already studying to be a male nurse, you can imagine how that introduction went, but it was clear, as my relationship with his daughter veered toward "in sickness and health," he wanted a relationship with me as his son, and I always kept him at arm's length. The only reason I came up with that makes any sense, as it was with my father-in-law and other men I respected, and I have been genuinely introspective about this, was that I was afraid to disappoint them. It was as if being in their company for a short time, saying the right things then disappearing before I screwed something up, would preserve what I perceived as a golden image. A psychiatrist in my second attempt at rehabilitation from myself diagnosed me with "impostor syndrome." I was afraid these men I respected would see me for the hack I was. I cut every conversation short for fear of saying something that would betray my air of being a stable human being. "Get over yourself," Kenny would have said. Kevin would have agreed. Easier said than done for me.

I was not born with a debilitating congenital syndrome. I did not grow up in a gangland steeped in terror and violence. I was not raised like a feral cat whose parents would rather leash in public than instill discipline. I am not a refugee from a war-torn country. I am not a victim of abuse, or anything else. It is easy to dismiss me as a privileged white boy blessed with more than most yet who was never satisfied. In rehabs and twelve-step meetings, I have bumped chairs with corporate executives and poured coffee for a dude with a face-tat who would put a bullet in you and be more concerned about finding the spent shell than your corpse. I have shaken hands with a woman who let her infant drown during tubby time while blitzed on an eight ball of heroin. I heard a woman speak at a meeting about nearly drinking herself to death because she did not get into her first choice of university. But whether we spent summers in an outhouse or grandma's shore house, we all wound up in the same place. Trauma is trauma.

It took three rehabs and over twenty years to realize the mind scars just as the body does. Those scabs, they catch on things, get torn off, and heal all wrong. My dad wanted to drink himself to death instead of being a dad—big deal. I was teased as a kid; join the club. I gave up on my dream of writing and working in film. I never even tried to fail; I just fell into a shame hole because I wanted it and never went after it. Boo-fucking-hoo. So, not much there to turn me into an addict who has altered lives and, potentially, could have ended others. But, besides addiction steeping in my genes, there was always this hole in my soul, bored deeper with each imagined failure. It is clear to me now what my role was in all of it—at least as clear as it has ever been—but that was not always so. I found a solution to a problem I did not have in drugs and alcohol. Then, that solution became the problem.

Trauma Is Trauma

We all endure pain and loss. We experience the vicarious trauma of those we care about, sitting with them in their pain and shame. Pain is energy, and like all energy, it is neither created nor destroyed, only transferred. We can bottle it up till it boils over, pass it on to others, or we can HURT (Harness UR Trauma). I told you my acronyms were cringy but bear with me. We addicts are a resourceful bunch. When we are not crafting crack pipes out of avocados, and crafting mind-shattering fictions that would make Christopher Nolan jealous, we are capable of remarkable achievements. I know a man who channeled the conviction he had copping and using to open a network of recovery houses to give men and women a chance to recover and get back on their feet. Two men I used to live with in one of these houses used their pain and anger to compose music, hurling insults at each other during the writing process. They went on to play shows together, enjoying success in doing something they loved. I know a "normie" who was nearly expelled from high school for running a locker thievery ring, among other destructive behaviors, likely the result of being raised in an alcoholic family. Years later, he is an elite special operations warrior as part of SEAL Team 6. We do not need such lofty goals through which to harness our potential. Today I wear the stigma of addiction like a badge of honor to show my two teenage children, who may one day suffer from the same disease, that it is possible to recover and be better for it.

That husky, sad little kid is now buried under two-hundred pounds of muscle. The insecure boy walks tall, even if he does give off an unapproachable demeanor at times. The man, who felt unease around men I feel are "better" than me, or at least seem more successful and content with themselves, persists, but the problem has been mitigated quite a bit by my need, and desire, to become an example rather than live with the fear of failing to follow another's. As a professional, I train others to save lives. As a father, I strive to help my children be content with their lives and, at the very least, avoid the mistakes I have made. As a person, I try to be better than I was the day before. We have an impact on people. Whether we act as an inspiration or a plague is entirely up to us.

Pain is inevitable; suffering is optional. HURT yourself and heal.

3

THE TALENTED MR. ELLIS

I take fire into my lungs with every breath. My heart tries to burst out of its cage. Every muscle in my body swells and screams in revolt. I want to die, and I have never felt so alive. I sit among seven other men trying to shed the remnants of boyhood feeling the same transcendent pain as we slice through the Schuylkill River in a sixty-foot racing shell. Our coxswain, Joe, squats in the stern, all 4'11" of him. He keeps us on course, calling out the race plan over tiny speakers in the boat.

Usually, Joe is cool as ice, but with just ten strokes to go in the race, we had a chance to beat our rival; as such, Joe was a tad unconventional. "First place! Give me FIRST FUCKING PLACE!" he roared. In that moment, I did not care if I died; I just wanted to leave every ounce of me on that river. Our enemies, in just as much pain as we were, watched with desperation, as we inched closer, despite giving their all. First, we take their souls, then we take their shirts; they were our trophies, the shirts, not the souls. After the race, in a time-honored tradition, the boats pull together just past the finish line. The losers remove their become, maybe it was best I stayed out of their way. T.O. defends our country as an elite member of the military, Vinny became the husband and father I should have aspired to, as well as my voice of reason, and Helene, our little Orphan Annie, is the prime example of "going with the flow."

Through herd mentality, and my ability to keep good grades and excel on a university rowing team, I regarded all my drinking and partying as standard college behavior. I saw no red flags waving. And that is the benchmark. With more than twenty million people in the world in the grips of addiction (oops, slipped in a stat), society says if you show up for work every day and only kick the dog on Tuesdays, then you are not an addict. When you get wasted halfway through an on-call shift at a hospital, as I have, that is a different story. It is all about how manageable your life is, or unmanageable, a word with which addicts are all too familiar. And after two years of higher education, though my life was not spinning out of control as it would a few years later, I was spinning my wheels in the mud regarding my future. When the thrill of the independence of new adulthood wears off, the existential crisis of figuring out what you want to be now that you are an adult, on paper at least, kicks in.

Outside of athletics and video games, the only thing I had an aptitude for was writing, at least that is what my high school English teachers told me. After struggling through a few writing classes at Rutgers, I decided it was not for me. Exercise Science was a major that was in vogue at the time and, given my passion for athletics, it seemed a good fit, until I heard through the resistance band that it was becoming an increasingly overcrowded field. Now I got worried. All my friends and teammates had a path forward except my best friend, Rob, who migrated with me from Philly to Jersey. We commiserated over our floundering futures one night during the weekly bash we threw every Thursday at our shitty off-campus house. Over the thump of mid-'90s hip-hop, some of the best beats ever pounding through speakers, Rob said he had a plan. I thought I was too drunk, or the bass was too loud, because what he said next sounded like "nursing." I had thought about doing many things in my life, but becoming a nurse was never one of them. Was a man even allowed to do that? You must understand, while men enjoy a robust and celebrated presence in nursing today, and I realize now, fighting a disease most of my life, it was exactly where I belonged, it was not that common twenty-five years ago. Tony Robbins once said, "In your life you need either inspiration or desperation." (Robbins, 2019) Back then, staring into the void of the rest of my life, I was not being picky. Once again, I was following someone else's plan, albeit someone in whom I had immense respect and trust. But this pattern of being reactive rather than proactive often did not serve me well. If we want to manage our own lives, we need to make the plans.

The next day, we spoke with the dean of Rutgers' nursing program; she practically fell off her chair when Rob and I expressed interest in enrolling. She explained there was a two-year wait list into Rutgers' prestigious program, but, in the interest of welcoming more males into the profession, she would grant us spots in the incumbent class if we could bang out a few prerequisite credits over the summer. It was a total diversity hire. And I was totally cool with it. So, taking a few steps out of my comfort zone the last few years showed me I was not as big a deal as I thought I was. We all need to get put in check from time to time. But perspective is like any expendable resource—there is far too little of it and we often waste what we have. I was looking at an amazing opportunity for a professional future and it just felt like I was settling for something less. But less than what? I have spent the last few years peering through the cold case files of my choices, reopening the investigation of my repeated implosions, and the only connection between these mind crimes was an insa-tiable need for more—more money, more stuff, more praise, more me. Addiction opens a hole we cannot ever fill, but, in sionist history, perhaps regret. My head still turned toward her; I slid my eyes back to the boys.

Twin Ford models. *No. Fucking. Way.*

"Which one is him?" I asked. C.C. walked away. Even Kenny and Kevin would have just been like, "Dude . . ." Yup, that happened, too. The checkout guy, probably wishing he could jump into the pool with them, looked at me with morbid curiosity. Pointing behind him I said, "She used to date one of them." He bagged up the shirt and handed it to me. His "have a good night, sir" dripped with sympathy. I never did wear that shirt. Okay, so she dated a supermodel that just so happened to be staring down at me now. A man confident in what he knew he had to offer would shrug it off; I was not that man. I think I would handle that situation better today.

I needed those "atta-boys" and "good jobs." The problem was, I never believed those statements. To me, they were "words of consolation." In my mind, I was a lost cause, but people felt bad for me, so they just said something nice. C.C. had already been with men who, at least to me, had a lot more going on but, as she has said many times since then, she chose me. It is not her fault that I never believed it. That became a pattern of poor thinking for me, always living in the shadow of something as quixotic as a supermodel to someone as real as a man I met in Honduras who had nothing but was grateful for everything. I could not achieve the impossible, nor could I be content with the inevitable. Remember, I am a normal kid with an embarrassment of privilege. So where did this defeatist thinking come from? One of the great mysteries of my mind, I gave up trying to figure it out long ago. All that mattered then was not letting the "crani" committee, the term I use for my persistent inner monologue, fuck up the best thing that ever happened to me.

As soon as you compare yourself to someone else, you have already lost. You think you are a social media maven? There are kids who cannot drive who have millions of Insta followers and who post heart emojis all over your ratioed tweets. You think your Rubi with thirty-five-inch KA02s and LEDs under the step-up is tight? You just saw a V8 329 Wrangler with a matte wrap zip by you without so much as a Jeep wave. Think your Keto for Kids regimen gets you Mom of the Year? Someone else bakes a daily serving of vegetables into gluten-free muffins their kids consume like crack. You think you destroyed your family because you are a chronic-relapsing alcoholic and drug addict? Your toddlers or your tweens or your teens or you ACOA's are getting along just fine without you. Believe me, I empathize, and I am guilty of chasing the carrots on sticks. That dude with the abs and vintage Tom Cruise grin forever falling back into that pool lived rent-free in my head for years and he never even knew I existed. Whatever I achieved was never enough. It could have been better; it should have been better. I should have been better. Where does this woeful lack of self-esteem come from? I used to care; I used to explore it in the safe havens of rehabs and with trusted friends who would not raise their eyebrows over the fact that I was jealous of a man I'd never met and harbored other unreasonable fears and resentments. Now I just stick with the facts of my life; whether I am sober or used, live in peace or in chaos, is entirely up to me.

During one of my self-imposed sabbaticals from nursing, I worked as a personal trainer. A youth filled with competitive swimming and rowing afforded me a decent physique; of course, I never thought it was good enough. Hearing this same lamentation from friends and strangers alike countless times, I think it is this dichotomous relationship with ourselves that lies at the root of our disease. We desire and require the positive reinforcement, but we do not believe it when we get it. Despite praise from men and women and even my own head nodding assessment in frequent visits to the mirror, I paled in comparison to muscle-bound legends and even contemporaries on my teams. The universal pursuit of perfection, where we strive to always be better, is a sound and sane concept, and a level of constructive self-criticism will always play an integral part—but in some of us it is broken. For me failure in an endeavor became a failure of self. That is an important difference.

Anyway, where was I? Right, I was a personal trainer, even though I was supposed to be a nurse. We will get to that. I had no experience as a PT, but given my nursing degree, an inherent knowledge of kinesiology from years of athletics and my bulging biceps got me the job. I realized with disappointment that training was 10 percent service, 90 percent sales and quickly became disenchanted with this exercise in exercise, but my time there provided me with a few services; I learned how to accept compliments and realized I had a knack for empowering others. Once, during a complimentary training session, paraphrasing a sales script, I asked a prospective client what he wanted to achieve. "I want to look like you," he said. He was not saying it to be nice. He meant it, and I was genuinely flattered. My response to him was, "You will never look like me." No, I didn't compensate for my insecurities by becoming a conceited dick. After he melted a bit, we went through a range of motion assessment where we compared how our bodies were constructed, pointed out his wide collar bones, low bicep tendon attachment, and the innate horse-shoe of his triceps and I explained that if he put the work in, he had the potential to look better than me. That was not just a sales ploy. That was a specific example, but its application to life is universal.

I could go the rest of this chapter cataloguing scenarios where we get so swept up trying to be someone else that we fall short of what we offer as ourselves. Nothing wrong in taking pride in who you are and what you do; just do not fall into the trap of thinking you do it best. You are not a special butterfly. As good as you think you are, there will always be someone better. Your best hope is to carve out a piece of peace in this life and just do you. Become your best self, stay in your lane, blaze your own trail, and you become the inspiration; you become the example. But with all things worth achieving, it takes work. It will take time, mistakes, and usually at least one other person to guide you. C.C. was that person for me. She was my muse, inspiring me to do the things I wanted to do. She was my greatest love and my greatest champion. It was as if just being around her, anything was possible. She gave me so many gifts—my children, my ambition, my home, how to love, and most importantly, how to be loved. C.C. just made me better. It is said that it is better to have loved and lost than to never have loved at all. Some days, when my heart is full and my eyes still get wet when I think of her and the pure love we had, I believe that; the other days, when I wish we never met, I respectfully disagree.

The shadow of my insecurities receded, and C.C. and I continued to fall madly in love. We met the parents and siblings; my friends and her friends became our friends, and we talked about getting married. We were a power couple in the making, the pride and joy of our family and friends. We were "C.C. & Sloane," spelled out proper; we were too big and too pure for a paparazzi portmanteau. Believe. She believed. I so badly wanted to. We graduated and life started to happen. We both moved back in with our parents. C.C., ever the independent, linked up with friends and GTFO ASAP. Never one to refuse coddling, I stayed in my childhood home until she and I were married. C.C. began a great career. I began my career as a registered nurse, which frankly, I did not like. It was not the work itself; I was fascinated by human physiology, pharmacology, and medical technology, and I enjoyed interacting with and helping the patients under my care. I was earning more money than I ever had, and I felt like a respected professional. I was relegated to working night shift, which was standard for a new nurse then, and it was fine at first. But as I creeped toward the decision that would irreparably change the course of my and C.C.'s life together, the "graveyard shift," as night shift is colloquially known, earned its reputation.

my high. After a short while my high became my norm. Everyone knew something was wrong with me, but I just perpetuated the assumption that the night shift was taking its toll. Binging on my reruns, I am surprised I got away with it as long as I did. A chronic opiate user is a rare thing as apathy and apnea quickly catch up with you, not to mention incarceration if you happen to steal for your supply. The first time I flirted with death I was lying in the bottom bunk in my childhood bedroom, in that liminal haze when I began to pass out from exhaustion and intoxication. I thought my father was there just looking at me. A dark haze was swallowing him up, turning him into a black, hooded figure, like a grim reaper. I remember gasping deep as light flooded the room again. My breath was coming forceful and deep and on its own. I had this familiar buzz in my head that I would get when I used to try and swim four laps underwater without surfacing and my dormant lungs would revolt against my ribs.

I stopped breathing.

Tolerance is inherently a good thing. Pain tolerance, exercise tolerance, tolerance of different races and customs, tolerance to bullshit, all aspects of a healthy mind and body. Tolerance to opiates, though, is not a good thing. I was steadily increasing my careful dosing, which meant I was taking more, to recapture that rapturous first euphoria, which I never would. The problem is that the garden of neurons in your brain responsible for keeping your lungs exchanging air gets blanketed with these delicious painkillers too. Pain is not all they kill. They also kill your ability to breathe. It is so insidious you do not realize you are not breathing. Maybe your brain will figure it out in the few minutes it takes for a cascade of little deaths to occur, leaving you a vegetable or going on into full cardiac arrest. The body and mind cannot live without oxygen. For a long time, I did not think mine could live without opiates.

Somehow, I would get more, yet not get caught or kill anyone or myself for almost two years, and I was making major decisions during that time, like asking C.C. to marry me and planning a future with her and enrolling in a master's program as a nurse anesthetist where I would gain access to the most powerful opiates in existence. To call that reckless is like calling a suicide bomber a dude holding sparklers; I was a criminal in every sense of the word. My rational mind was screaming at me to stop, but all I heard was a whisper. I tried a few times, going so far as tossing my pilfered stash in the trash. Within hours, I was sifting through junk mail and half-eaten food to salvage every precious pill.

"The chains of addiction are too weak to be felt until they are too strong to break." (Burne, 1847)I was locked in the deadly triad of obsession, craving, and compulsion and I had no idea how to get out. I should have asked for help. C.C. had no idea what was happening, but she would have understood; I never doubted her loyalty to me or her love. I told myself I did not want to disappoint her or my family; I did not want to tarnish my golden image. But that was all bullshit. Turning myself in meant I would have to stop, and I was not ready. I thought of my dad, sitting in the bar all those years ago, me wondering why he could not stop; I finally knew.

regard for our behavior while our ego has the reins. Everything else comes after our needs and wants, but even those "phantom" choices we make have real consequences. Be it by design or compulsion, regardless of how infallible or ill-fated we think we are, we reap what we sow.

"Betrayed" by my work wives. Terry, Iris, and Gloria trolled the floor, trying to stifle the hurried squeak-walk of their clogs echoing through the halls, interviewing patients to see if their perceived pain matched up with my record of it. It did not. I like to think they struggled with what to do next. We had been friends for years. We did potlucks, went out for drinks, and shared the singular stress of being a registered nurse. The cynical bastard in me would say nurses will eat their own as they always have. The professional name tag pinched on my scrubs reminded me they had an obligation to report me or risk their own licenses. My tattered inner empath understood they were not doing this to me; they were doing it *for* me. They were going to end my career to save my life. While the first group of my reluctant saviors, and the many to follow in the coming years, likely made a clear, albeit difficult, decision, my "crani-committee" disagreed.

The next morning, after my commute home, I popped some pills and was deciding how to misspend my day when I got a call from my supervisor. She said she was sorry to wake me. She said I needed to make the hour trek back to work to answer some questions. In that whimpering voice of a child caught with his hand in the cookie jar, or narc box, as it were, I asked if everything was okay. I knew it was not. She just said, "We need you to come back." My dad swing-walked into my room with a casual horror as I hung up the phone, that molded mask of bewilderment with sparks of recognition in place. I looked at him then flicked my eyes to his left into my vanity mirror. The resemblance was uncanny. When he would see me, he would call out one of a half dozen greetings. "Beautiful day," he bellowed. Always facts, Dad. I wish I could agree.

When I got back to the hospital, trussed up in a shirt and tie and my bladder distended with a gallon of water, my union rep sat me down and showed me the controlled substance ledger. All the suspect entries with my signature were highlighted. The page was mostly yellow. The rep explained that what I was being accused of "could affect your entire future." I will never forget the terror of those words. I never wanted to feel that way again. Of course, over the next twenty years, this became a familiar dread. Months later, when I returned to that hospital, invited back in my first desperation gig as a unit secretary, I pulled Terry aside and thanked her for saving my life; she would not be the last person to do so. But right then, feeling the mortal weight of those words, sinking in the quicksand of my consequences, I wanted to pile her and her eight kids into a yellow bus and send it off a cliff.

May 25, 2001, is the only day of my life where, save for the first few minutes of those twenty-fours where I reflected on the last few months that brought us here, I was exactly where I was supposed to be. It was the only day where it was not pain or regret or shame that forced me into the present. There was none of the shame of watching C.C. wrestle for months with doubt amid the fallout of my betrayal of her love and trust. There was none of the fear of starting from scratch, the gleaming future we were building together buried under the weight of my actions. There was just me and C.C. and the people we loved most in life celebrating us. I was living every moment as it occurred because that was exactly what I wanted; it was the most perfect day of my life. It was the day we got married.

A soft sun woke the day, and I awoke in my childhood bedroom in the bottom bunk as I had for most of my life. Though this was not the last time I would wake up there, it is the last time this would truly be my home. Things were about to change in a big way. I was excited and scared. I lay for a little while, thinking about how much had already changed, like, for instance, I was still lying in a bunk staring at Star Wars wallpaper rather than the cold steel of a jail cell. All told, I was let off lightly. The hospital was mandated to report me to the Board of Nursing, which summarily suspended my license to practice nursing for three years. The hospital did not press charges and no legal action was taken; I was even offered a position as a unit clerk to keep me afloat. Then, I considered myself fortunate. The toughest part was breaking the news to my two favorite ladies: C.C. and my mom. They took it well, all things considered, but eventually they asked that insoluble question: "Why?" C.C. spent the next few weeks doing some major soul-searching. We were getting married in just under four months and we had to decide if we should stay the course—well, she had to decide; I had no other course.

Those first weeks, C.C. struggled every day to understand how I could invest so much in my selfish decisions rather than our future. She understood I was sick, that "choice" was a relative term when it came to my actions, but she needed the "why." She asked if it was her, if my job and commute was getting to me, or if "till death do us part" was too much of a commitment. It was all of it and none of it; whatever reason I had for swallowing those first few pills no longer mattered after I did. After that, it was all about recapturing that seminal, perfect euphoria. I still remember the two of us sitting with my mom, a woman who knew all too well the stress and sacrifice of staying with a man who was a slave to addiction. C.C. was asking for her perspective; I was begging C.C. to stay with me; it would not be the last time I did.

We sat down with the pastor of C.C.'s church, the man who was to marry us, to get his perspective. This devout man of God spent the first half of our session together trying to understand why I would take a painkiller if I was not in pain. After chalking it up to sins of the secular, in a tone full of compassion, he told us if we truly wanted to be together, love and prayer conquer all. I was not sold on the prayer part, but I knew beyond any doubt that I loved C.C. and I could not imagine living my life without her. I am not one of those guys who just assumed he would have the status quo wife and kids one day; it was never something I thought about or wanted. She helped me see the beauty of a life like that. I proposed to her and started a family with her because of her; because she gave me something I never knew I needed or wanted.

The rules of sobriety include choosing a higher power to believe in, if only so we understand there is something greater than us. Most choose a god of their understanding. I know a woman who chose waterfalls as hers, citing the power and majesty of Niagara Falls, which could pound you to a pulp; that works. Even before deciding to go through with our wedding, C.C. was my higher power. I was in awe of her since we met. She had the strength and resilience of my mother interwoven with a confidence, assertiveness, and sex appeal I had never known in a woman, but she was much more than that. She seemed to have the answers to everything; she was my guide to life, and I relied on her for almost everything. C.C. always reminded me during our life together that she chose me; I chose her, too, but I needed her more. In C.C., all things were possible. And throughout our life, I would ask for her guidance and beg her forgiveness with the earnestness of any prayer, genuflected and humble. The day she answered my prayer to become my bride, I placed her on her pedestal; I held her up because I aspired to be her, to gain her strength. I believed in her to guide us, to guide me, to always be there when I fell. She was my North Star, my mainsail, and my rudder.

A word of advice—do not ever do this to someone. Deifying another person, likening them to an omnipotent savior, an elemental force, or an ex machina that solves all your problems, is unfair to them and creates unrealistic expectations. We should not seek a savior; we should seek a partner. A relationship works both ways; we take what is offered and we give of ourselves in return. When we place a partner above us, as I did, a vicious cycle of redemption and resentment ensues; it is inevitable and insidious and defeats the purpose of a loving relationship. Your partner should be your equal, not your god.

The day of the wedding was a fairy tale. It was the best wedding I had ever attended, and not just because it was mine and C.C.'s. If you are married, you are probably saying, "Well, my day was better." Nope. It wasn't. This wedding was perfect. Everything about it, from the ceremony in a Romanesque church, to being showered with confetti and rose petals during our procession outside as husband and wife for the first time, to our reception in a nineteenth-century country estate replete with Victorian splendor, Old World grace, and contemporary spirit, tucked behind a wall of hedgerows; it was a true diamond in the rough of the Neast. Even our engagement in Ireland, more than a year prior, was out of a fantasy novel. I walked around for four days with C.C.'s ring taped to the inside of my thigh to preserve the surprise. We visited the ruin of the Rock of Cashel, the most impressive cluster of medieval buildings in the Emerald Isle, set on a dramatic outcrop of limestone in the Golden Vale. Under the only surviving Romanesque fresco in Ireland, I dropped to my knee, took her hand, and asked her to marry me. I was never more excited to do anything than give her that ring.

I wanted it to be a normal wedding day, but I was afraid the emotional tide of what happened four months ago would tug at the joy of it. It was there, but it poured out as elation in the form of a jig, danced to the tune of a live Irish band. It was in the hugs, held for a few moments longer; it was in the tender, tearful smiles from family, friends, and even the bartenders and white-gloved waitstaff gathered in a circle for an encore of our dance under an ornate indoor pergola that ended the evening. It was fucking perfect.

Just ask any of the more than two hundred souls in attendance. On our video, friends and family watching us dance, there was real love in their eyes as they held each other and swayed along with us. Everyone from our parents to our siblings, to our families, our friends, to my six cousins on my grandmother's side who we invited as a courtesy but never thought would come, watched us with love and awe. They believed in us. They knew if anyone could get through this and be stronger for it, it was C.C. and Sloane. It was supposed to be a story of redemption, of breaking the cycle, of a love so pure it makes you cry. This was the way everyone should feel, and that day I felt everything was going to be okay. Believe. I so wanted to believe. Everyone deserves a second chance, but not a third, or more, as I have been given, especially when those chances evoke more hubris than humility, as they have in me. That day was the best chance I would ever have to live up to the fairy tale. My terminally unique solution for life was terminally flawed, so I found a new solution; her name is C.C. Ellis.

You Are Not a Special Butterfly

To be extraordinary, we first must achieve ordinary. We are never as good as we think we are, nor are we as bad. A friend in sobriety once told me, "God doesn't make trash." Some days, it is hard to agree with that, but I understood why she said it to me. When shame comes calling after failing to be your best yet again, remember we are not perfect and never will be.

We must move past who we were. We are not slaves to our genetics. We are not our labels. We are not our socioeconomic status. We are not our Facebook "likes." We are not terminally unique; we are not special butterflies; we are MOTHS (Move On to a Higher Self). Take your own reins; don't be yanked by them. We spend so much time trying to be what we think we should be, we forget who we want to be. There is love and compassion and purpose all around us. Life will happen and we can conform to it, from anything is that, even though we are clean, when we are in that limbo between the twilight period after we get off our drugs of choice and when our natural painkillers kick back in, the enemy still has the advantage. When we first get sober, everything just feels . . . less. In the extremes of active addiction, it was all or nothing. I either loved the world or I hated it. When I was using, I felt like a part of the world, the dumped dopamine from my pills rendering all those vibrant details you could never admire while sober. The way the world seemed to spin just that little bit slower, you notice things you otherwise never would. Everything just seemed more interesting. If I had not gotten my standard rations for the day, my fix, the world was a braying, out-of-tune instrument; it was a rabid kiosk salesperson in the mall scurrying out to ruin your day. The world was that asshole two rows behind you in the movie theater having a phone conversation on speaker; it was a peloton of middle-aged cyclists, donned in caricatural performance gear, blocking traffic on a one-lane road for their "Tour de Suburb." Fuck the world. Today, more than four years sober, depending on the circumstance, I sway somewhere in between these extremes.

Internally, it is our physiology righting itself, the production of our natural endorphins coming back online after a time of dormancy and likely mild clinical depression. Externally, the world seems foreign, like we no longer belong to it. The world kept spinning while we stayed in our own present—the curse of emotional stagnation while in active addition; everything stops except our need to feed. We come out of it with a kind of shell shock as our brain recalibrates to a life we left behind.

THOUGH THIS WAS a rehab primarily designed for treating drug and alcohol addiction, anyone with an intolerance to their own life could benefit from it. The rooms were all set up with a ring of chairs, their inhabitants a melting pot of age, race, and circumstance. Whether you were there at the insistence of an employer, spouse, or state, there was one common theme among us— everyone in that joint got caught. There was the occasional good egg that saw their life had become unmanageable and checked themselves in, but that was a rare occurrence. After you get over acting like the petulant child being someplace you do not want to be, there is a wealth of knowledge you can glean in a place like this. As I watched the wind carve snow drifts through the window, a man came in and greeted me with a smile. "Hey, I'm Nick," he said. Nick, a driver for FedEx, used to snort lines of cocaine off packages in the back of the delivery truck. "This your first rehab?" asked Nick. I paused, not understanding the question. *Yeah, first and last,* I thought. "People do this more than once?" I asked out loud. Nick made with a *you have a lot to learn* snort. "Yeah, man," he said, chuckling. "Third DUI for me, third treatment." I hoped the shock and disgust I felt did not show on my face. I just could not comprehend it. With the consequences of my diversion and abuse of Percocet from the hospital in which I worked as a registered nurse at the time still raining down around me and my family, I could not imagine going through all this again, let alone a third time (or a four-teenth, the most rehab stints I have heard one going through to date).

Nick was one of a cast of colorful characters I met in my recovery tour. Joanne picked dead cigarettes out of the trash, sparking the hope, and the butt, that there was a puff left when her Adderall ran out. Jen was a dual diagnosis, substance abuse and bipolar disorder—the two often share a bed together. Jen was here in lieu of a prison cell after she broke the jaw of another driver in the battle for a parking space at Walmart. We were all "outies," outpatients that commuted to the site each day. We were joined every morning by the "innies," inpatients that were housed on-site and escorted to our groups. These were the "shot-out" dregs of humanity I had envisioned when signing on; years to find that euphoria. The gravity of temptation grew heavier every year.

How could I tell C.C. that? How could I let her know after what I had put her through and the months of treatment and vows I swore that I missed the thing that nearly destroyed our life together? I could not. And, like all lost things, I thought time would do its thing and I would get over it. So, even when I was not fine, I was fine.* I kept my masks handy, kept "faking" it until that day came, passively defending, trying to starve out the demons beyond the wall. Some enemies have the patience of the pyramids.

We need victories to keep up hope, and we had enjoyed a steady string of them. C.C. continued to climb the corporate ladder, and I began my studies as an anesthetist, turning a regrettable career decision into one I was genuinely excited about. Then, our greatest victory yet—we were graced with our daughter, Cleo Ellis, in 2003. There is the deepest love you can feel for another, that absolute conviction that you would do anything for them, and then there was this. All the bullshit I was obsessing over, my sanctions with the nursing board, the lingering pill-shaped hole in my soul, gone. My God, what I felt that day. Her lying on a tiny warming table moments after coming into the world, a heart-shaped temperature probe over her belly button. She finally settled, her war cries calming to a coo. I stroked her impossibly soft skin; she looked at me and I said, "I will always be here for you." A promise. I meant that. I still do, and I am still here to make good on it.

I was proud to introduce her to our families, especially my dad and my grandmother. I have a picture of my dad holding her. I cannot recall if he had held a baby since my siblings and I were that small, but I will never forget his vacant eyes lighting up, his posture strong and his loving grip on Cleo. It seemed to bring him a peace he had not known for a long time. And I am glad my grandmother got to meet her; sadly, my grandfather, the great old oak himself, passed earlier that year. He grumbled and groaned to the end, but he lived a good long life and he died peacefully in his sleep. Cleo was her first grandchild and would be her only one. My grandmother died a year later from complications from a pulmonary embolism, though I think it was of a broken heart. She and my grandfather were married just over fifty years, a rare thing even then, let alone today. Me, C.C., my parents, and siblings were honored to attend dinner with them on their fiftieth anniversary. In the middle of the celebration, my grandfather stood up and serenaded my grandmother in one of the most endearing displays of love I have ever seen. In that moment, they were the two kids who fell in love a half-century before. I had that kind of love.

After C.C. and I were married and began growing our life together, I barely saw my dad. Like the customary splitting of assets in a divorce, you split family holidays while still married. Easter with my family, Thanksgiving with hers, Christmas Eve with mine, New Year's Day with hers, flip flop the following year, flop flip the year after, and on and on it went. There was the occasional birthday and hallmark holidays but beyond that our life was the priority. I was a father now and my focus was on being a better one than he was. I had not thought of him much in the weeks leading up to his death. He had been the walking dead for years, his mind drowning in dementia, his body failing more every year. But I had not thought of him because I had not thought of much beside myself. I had spent most of that day in class, working toward my degree. I had planned to hit the gym or do something besides heading straight home after when I got a call from C.C. asking when I would be home. She did not give a reason and I did not ask. Reluctantly, I went straight home. C.C. practically met me at the door. Beautiful C.C.. Her face hung with sadness and concern; in the years to come, it would be streaked with tears many times, it would contort in anger, fear, and desperation, and finally smooth in resignation—always

7

INCAPABLE

San Pedro Sula, Honduras, looks like most third-world urban villages. A sprawl of patchwork buildings and garish logos advertise things no one there could afford. Residents seem to wander without much purpose. A shirtless middle-aged man drags a dead dog behind him. Commuters on mopeds share the road with horse-drawn carriages. Starved livestock roam the countryside. Hospital El Progresso, or "Un Progresso," as it came to be known in our week there, less dilapidated than neighboring structures, squats behind a gate with guards. We pull into lines of sick and weary Hondurans, their eyes following our vans. We form a chain and unload our equipment through a window. The ER is a twisting corridor littered with sick and desperate patients and their families, days of dirty food plates stacked beside them on their stretchers. All eyes are on us as we carefully navigate the labyrinth of misery—tattered bandages hanging from limbs, heads, and torsos, they turn toward us as we walk by, hoping for us to grasp their hands and heal their pain. Others have no hands to reach out, as they've been hacked off with machetes, the weapon of choice of gangs from nearby Tegucigalpa, the capital of the republic and the capital of crime. Harrowing and humbling, Honduras.

By 2013, I had been practicing as a nurse anesthetist for seven years at a major hospital specializing in all types of surgical specialties. As such, I felt ready for most situations and not just with respect to medicine and healthcare. As anesthetists we were afforded much more autonomy as nurses, making decisions we were unable to when we had fewer letters after our name. We were more respected by surgeons and physicians, often deferred to when a patient's airway was compromised, and drew looks of admiration and jealousy from contemporaries in nursing. A certified registered nurse anesthetist (CRNA) was a coveted role for many and a difficult program of study, and I felt pride and gratitude in getting through it. I was making more money than I ever thought I would, finally felt appreciated as a nurse, and for a man with lingering self-esteem issues, this role did wonders for my ego. And by "wonders," I mean ballooned it into the stratosphere.

My apologies for the *Westworld--esque* quantum leap in the story but I am getting to the good parts and want to save enough space. You did not miss much. To summarize the gap, C.C. and I were achieving everything we dreamed and more. We settled into our dream home, complete with the 1.5 acres of land, picket fence, detached barn, and country colonial charm, continued to grow as a financial power couple, bought a vacation home, and added Adam Ellis to our happy little family in 2007. Oh, Adam. If only you and your sister could have stayed children forever. I was probably at my best when they were young. In many ways, I have always been a child at heart; I am still. Having permission to be a child with them was a dream come true for me. They have outgrown me over the last few years, and I have struggled with that, especially being away from them for most of each week, a result of my incurred exile. Today, I feel we share a unique bond, one that gives me such peace and pride even amidst my darkest descents. I think of them; the rest is easy. There is still much more to come on my favorite people on this earth. Stay tuned. And, of course, my keelhauling down the center of a provincial suburb at the hands of yuppie douchebags and my own stupidity happened during this time of peace and prosperity as well.

Back to my expanding head. I was never a conceited person. I never cared much for shows of wealth, mostly because I never had any, but even though we cracked the upper crust, save for some lavish vacations and our home, we never spent above our means. But after working in my capacity as a CRNA for years, side by side with surgeons and anesthesiologists, a subtle inferiority complex seeped in. For me, it became hard to focus on what I had when these men and women had so much more. They did not overtly flaunt their wealth—well, some did, but that is to be expected. Some of these docs were like rappers who came from nothing, hit it big, and now have gold-plated steering wheels because they can. To my knowledge, none of my colleagues had gold-plated steering wheels, but I started to resent the nonchalance of their parading, inviting coworking hunters to shoot game *on their property*, and comparing the tacit idles of their hybrid Porches and electric Beamers; suddenly, my push-start Nissan was not all that. Someone with self-confidence, someone who knew who they were, someone with real gratitude would have been pleasant enough to nod, smile, and move on. I was not that someone.

In the meantime, my addiction, or let us just cut the shit and call it "I," had been conspiring with myself, cultivating a campaign of terror on my soul the likes of which I could not fathom. But I was fine.* So, I started to spend. They were small things, at first. Video games, home theater equipment, high-end collectibles based on favorite movie and comic franchises. I began working out again consistently, so I got into bodybuilding supplements. But for every good habit I set in place, a half dozen more marred its surface before it cured. Soon, my inner addict started to run with it. My frivolous purchases compounded so much that I opened a separate bank account, of which C.C. was unaware, siphoning off money from my check each month to support my secret spending. In truth, the secrecy of the whole thing became a high, a self-funded trust that carried as much betrayal as a tryst. In my last rehab, Warren, one of my favorite people and the "Chuck D" of drug counselors, once said, "If you want to end yourself and give the devil a subsidy, then shut your mouth and 'Don't tell nobody.'" I love that guy. Wise words that I likely would have ignored even then as I conspired with myself. I developed a taste for expensive craft beer and bought it by the cases. When that was not enough, I looked to our detached barn, and turned it into a full bar.

It was a plywood canvas with copper piping snaking through the walls used as conduits for the former owner's various pneumatic tools. I left them intact to preserve the industrial feel. I installed a chair rail around the five-hundred-square-foot interior, glued up faux-tin tiles along the bottom third, and painted the walls above the rail a kelly green. Photos and aluminum beer signs adorned the walls; my father's old pool table found a new home; even an authentic *Street Fighter II* arcade cabinet sat in a corner. It became a centerpiece for our annual fall Ogtoberfest bash and a vault for day-drinking on my days off. My brother-in-law loaned me a gorgeous mahogany bar top transplanted from a restaurant he used to own and, before that, if his father is to be believed, once adorned a pub in Chicago owned by one Al Capone. I installed a mini fridge that held two sixtel kegs full of potent craft beer. I drilled a hole through the top, dropped two tap lines down from the nickel-plated tap tower drilled into Al's bar top, and sealed up the lines and holes with foam insulation and foil tape. My vainglorious cherry on top? Custom tap handles chased down on eBay and other niche online vendors. If the level of detail sounds over the top it is because I was going over the top, becoming obsessed with all my hobbies, always adding more to fill that bottomless hole.

Stacee, a dear friend and counselor by trade, once explained the concept of "scarcity" to me. It is a state of mind in which, despite all we have in our lives, we focus on what we lack. Despite all the good that has happened, we obsess over the bad that could. I had so many gifts. A loving marriage, two beautiful, healthy children, an amazing career, the means to do basically whatever we wanted. I had more than most would in a lifetime. I had no right to be asking myself, "Is this all there is?" But I asked it anyway. "Scarcity" is universal enough that it has been researched and immortalized in textbooks, but for the terminally unique like me, it is a desolate place to be.

That brings us back to Honduras. C.C. and I had already done some volunteer work in the community, providing a Pre-Cana class to couples getting married in the Catholic Church. It was during this experience, as C.C. and I explored the evolution of our relationship, that we came up with what we thought was a clever metaphor of an amusement park. She was the sky car, affording a constant vista over our life. With all my ups and downs, I was the roller coaster. It was a beautiful experience and I wanted to do more related to my profession, especially after disenchantment had begun to set in. I embarked with two other CRNAs, a surgical team, and a medical team to the impoverished country hoping to find something spiritual and real. It was an incredible experience. Some cases I would work with my predominately English-speaking team, and during others, I was the only practitioner that did not speak Spanish, yet we all did what we do best in any language. The thrill of absolute autonomy in practice, and doing my job in a place whose vernacular, customs, and landscape were so foreign yet rendered so familiar by the universal language of medicine, was almost intoxicating . . . in a good way. Natives walked in on legs blackened and rotted from lack of circulation, with gallbladders cobbled with stones and ready to burst. A right in the U.S., proper healthcare is a luxury in Honduras. In the States, most people would never progress to such a sorry state, but here, those seeking care could not do so until they scraped together enough Lempira, the Honduran currency, to afford their own medical supplies. They dragged themselves in, toting their own sterile gowns and dressings, elated to finally have fractured bones mended and infection drained from their bodies.

"They are poor, but they are happy," mused Rudy, as we shared a beer looking out over a blighted vista of brown fields and half-built shacks from the perch of our guarded compound. I worked with Rudy back home. He was one of our orthopedic technicians, an Everyman who assisted in setting bones and suturing among other tasks and, as Spanish was his native tongue, here in Honduras, his skill as a translator was invaluable. Before he was forced out of his home in Bolivia, years prior, Rudy was a cardiothoracic surgeon. I do not know the details, but as I understand it, Rudy took his family and fled his native country amid a violent coup in Bolivia against doctors and healthcare workers. He did what a good man and father does—he took what was necessary and got to safety. Of course, the first world will give you asylum, but will never let you forget your third-world roots. Without the means or time to complete a decade of education and training to be declared a medical doctor in the U.S., Rudy could only use his surgical skill in a non-licensed capacity. If this blatant disrespect seethed within him, Rudy never showed an iota of ire.

In my years working with him, I never knew a more jovial and grateful person. This was a man at peace with his decisions and himself. At that moment, as we watched the destitute citizens of San Pedro Sula live that day as if it were their last, Rudy knew exactly how they felt. God, I wanted that. I craved the tranquility on his face, the bucolic repose of those people with nothing but content they had everything. A few more days here, I thought I might get it. That week, I felt lighter, as if my faceless doubts and fears, my scarcity, were held at the border. There was just us, them and the purity of people helping people. I tried so hard to hold onto that after I got home, that new perspective, that spiritual awakening all lost souls seek so desperately. For a time, everything seemed more vibrant, from the beautiful innocence of my children to C.C.'s patient love, even to my daily commute to work. Everything just seemed more interesting; nothing was trivial. Sound familiar? As I would prove to myself many times since then, I was incapable of holding on to the transcendent gifts of these experiences, inevitably letting the daily grind pulverize them into shimmering sand. They slip through my fingers, leaving only a distant gleam, their lessons too dull to be seen when my mind starts to churn.

Each night, exhausted and elated, we were rewarded with a delicious meal provided by the house staff—Honduran baleadas; Korean bibimbap, as our host was a Korean physician by way of Miami; and libations, smuggled in by us, of course. Every night, we would have a few drinks before bed, discussing the day, getting to know more about each other. For most, it was liquid decompression, venting out the rest of the stress and adrenaline of what were unprecedented experiences for many of us. For me, it was a welcome end to each day, but I quickly got accustomed to the subtle calm alcohol affords, and each I night craved camaraderie less and that familiar fuzz more. Keep your friends close and your enemies closer, indeed.

Back in rehab, we learned about the dreaded "I Nevers," taunts the enemy uses to psych us out. At least "I never missed work because I was too drunk," "I never blacked out," "I never drove drunk with my kids in the car, while watching their cartoons" . . . until I did. Make a list of all the things you could never imagine doing then wake up in horror as you check another one off. After returning home, I started to drink more steadily, chasing those moments of liquid peace, still trying to reclaim that lost euphoria again. Over the next year and a half, I continued to work without incident. Me, C.C., Cleo, and Adam, the "Ellis 4," lived and loved and went on vacations and we continued to be the perfect little family on the outside. Everything was fine. I was fine.* Except I was not. As always, C.C. was patient and forgiving of my impulsive and selfish actions. She believed in me and our love for each other. What she did not understand she always tried to accept and give me the strange space I needed. But one can only bend so far before they break. I was on a "post-call" day, a day off after a twenty-four-hour shift. I enjoyed one of these free days once a week where I would "rest" while C.C. was at work and the kids were at school or aftercare. It was always my role to pick them up and get them home for dinner. By now, my day drink approached a fifth of vodka, concealed in a water bottle. I chose vodka over beer on the days, times, and situations in which I should not be drinking, which were all of them, because I was under the false notion it had no smell—not to me, at least. You cannot smell your own body odor, but everyone else can. You do not feel the effects of a ton of bricks you drop in a puddle, but whatever is in it sure does.

I startled awake on our office/guest room floor to a slamming door and C.C. yelling my name. I grabbed my phone, which showed missed texts and calls and the time: 5:20 p.m. I was supposed to have my children in the car by four thirty. "At least I never got drunk and left my kids at daycare." Until I did. Her feet pounded across the wood floor and up the stairs as I scrambled to look like I was not plastered in daylight when I should be making my kids dinner. The look on her face. Without a word she left to do what I should have done. I called her; she answered. For the thousandth time, I apologized and groveled and asked how I could make it better, and for the thousandth time she listened patiently and answered in an even tone, "Nothing." The next day, after work, was my first official intervention. C.C. came home early before the kids were done with school, aimed her beautiful blue eyes at my bullshit brown ones, and said one word: "Truth." That word should not instill the fear in me that it does.

lives. I look back now on the journal I kept of that time. Thirty days, thirty entries full of flowery prose and naivety, but also the instructions of a way of thinking it would take another five years to adopt as my own. Some entries had a tingle of truth, where pure emotion bled onto the page along with lots of empty promises I never upheld. I look at it now and I am just sad I failed to become the man I detailed in those pages. I remember much about that month. The men and women I befriended, most there because they got caught but willing to become better, I came to care for very much, especially Kathleen. She was also a nurse. We came to share a special bond and kind of a platonic love for each other. We wanted each other to succeed at life. She was discharged from Livengrin a few days before me but left me a note before she did. I still have it and unfold it whenever the darkness is at its worst. It is nearly unreadable from my excessive handling of it.

There was Sheila, a no-bullshit counselor who first helped me understand my war was in my head and the true enemy was not addiction, but me. But just understanding is not believing. There was my squad in "G-House," the recovery dorm I was placed in, where we shared war stories and our hopes of a future free of strife. We came up with a war cry with which we would begin and end every day: "Fuck the Zero." This referred to counting our days of sobriety. We were always either heading toward recovery or relapse, which would bring those hard-won days down to zero. Then there was Charlie, a grizzled recovery vet and patient care technician who rocked suspenders and a bow tie and spat truths older than most of us under his care. Charlie always had questions and he challenged us to find the answers. My favorite was "You know the difference between running your life and ruining it?" I did not know the answer. He put his hand on my shoulder and looked at me over his readers with a grandfather's love. "I," he said. But what I remember most about Livengrin were the dreams.

My second night in G-house, I saw my father under a giant oak tree. He was smoothing his hands across the gnarled roots and knots on its shaft. When he saw me, his eyes clear, he gave a big smile and just said, "You're all right, buddy." Never questions, just facts. In another, maybe a week later, he was under the same tree, and we sat. My father and I sat together and just talked. I do not even know what we talked about. In most of my dreams that I could remember over the last few years, there was always the shadow of something sliding over me. The shuffling slow-walk of a slasher-movie juggernaut, the creak of wings—sometimes was very distant, barely a whisper; other times, there was breath on my neck. Under that tree, there was none of that. I just remember being next to him, the rich tenor of his voice and his laugh, the joyful decrescendo. My dad was more alive and happier than I ever saw him when he was alive. I wanted that. I wanted him. I did not even know how much I missed him.

I came home lighter, not unlike my return from Honduras. C.C. was there to meet me at the door where she dropped me off a month ago, hoping to get her husband back. I turned my phone on for the first time in thirty days and it lit up with a string of texts, words of affirmation and support, speaking my language. She took my hand in hers and smiled at me. She said she was looking forward to having us whole and happy again in this "new normal." I never did like that word, "normal," but I was tired of fighting this war. It was a war I could never win, only surrender the outcome.

Know Your Enemy

THIS WAS a lesson I ignored for too long. We all have that someone or something that kills us every time. In AA, we call them "People, Places, and Things"—the "Big 3," the unholy trinity of blind spots and chinks in our armor that take us out.

They can take the form of external demons and dalliances or internal defects of character. A former sponsor once told me my "person" was me, my "place" was my mind, and my "thing" was my ego. I scoffed at the assessment at the time, but my actions and consequences, my failure to know my enemy and myself, has undone me every time. I imagine many of us are our own worst enemies. So, what happens when, after thinking we were the protagonist in our own lives, we realize we are the antagonist? How do we defeat ourselves? We PLAN.

PICK YOUR BATTLES—Do not nitpick everything that is wrong with your world; conserve your energy for the things that really matter.

Lighten Your Load—We all likely have too much going on in our lives. Cut out what is not necessary.

Ask for Help—I never did until it was too late. We all have someone we can reach out to. If you are not, ask yourself why.

No to the Zero—Or Fuck the Zero, if you prefer, but it does not roll off the tongue as well. Do not go backwards—stay away from the "Big 3." You keep hanging around a barbershop, you are eventually going to get a haircut.

8

COMPLIANCE FICTION

Adam grins as the spinning fury from twin Fragnarok™ canons pulses down his arms. It almost tickles, like trying to withstand the "shock" from that old arcade game where you grip two furiously vibrating silver handles for as long as you could. Befitting its apocalyptic moniker, the titular Fragnarok™ is a prototype "Gatling railgun," sporting six sets of electromagnetic propulsion-powered ultanium© rails on oscillating rotors capable of delivering depleted uranium slugs at 4,000 RPM with a top speed of 3 km/second. Adam has two of these shredding a towering horror show before him; a massive, shambling murder machine, and all it is doing is pissing it off.

A battered exoskeleton, nothing more than a mess of neosteel beams and pistons molded to roughly accommodate the average human body and welded together, offers Adam as much protection as a mesh condom. Acting as little more than a scaffold for the guns that the eggheads back in R and D postulate will hold together, Adam plods along in his "suicide suit," to which he cynically refers to as the shell, with surprising grace along the war-torn planet, adjusting his angles of fire on the monstrosity, a

writhing where we caged them. I would do anything for my children. I would cut the beating heart from my chest without anesthesia and without hesitation if it meant they would live on another day. But I could not stay sober for them. I could not stay sober for my marriage or my career or an auditorium full of friends and family that wanted nothing but to see me healthy and happy. I could not get clean because, despite all my words and promises and bullshit, I did not want to. Everyone knew that but me.

The lies we tell ourselves run deeper than the sea. And just as we cannot make lasting changes in ourselves without our own permission, we cannot expect anyone to be our savior even if they want to be. I always expected C.C. to be there and pick up the pieces of me when I would inevitably shatter again. It was worse than selfish; it was irresponsible and cruel, even if I did not intend it to be. No one should have to compromise their own happiness to improve yours. Nothing is trivial, from selfless acts to selfish ones, to the promises we make and break, to the vows and lies we swear with straight faces. The little white lies we tell others and ourselves clump on top of each other like the steady dribble of wet sand you would pour into a crappy castle on the beach. A seed is one of the most trivial things there is at first glance. But a seed can germinate into something as epic as a redwood tree given the time. I planted a seed before I left Livengrin, one that would grow into something awful.

You do not have to frequent twelve-step meetings, where the aphorism "One Day at a Time" is proudly displayed; it is a common piece of wisdom. Recovery literature expounds upon that precept, cautioning against focusing on two days, yesterday and tomorrow. (SEPIA, 2022) I was still regretting my mistakes of the past and fearing a future I knew nothing about instead of devoting myself to today. I was trying to digest the half-lifetime I had left in one sitting, chewing over an existence free of my secret solutions. I emptied my pockets, and everything was on the table now—drugs, money, time, and now my booze. I had nothing left to hide behind and I was having a hard time getting used to that. No one can process the rest of their life in a car ride home; that is why we do it "one day a time." That sounded too tedious to me, so I stuck to my grand, sweeping timeline, letting the weeks and months fall off the calendar, biding my time. Maybe I would make sobriety a way of life; maybe I would find another solution, one I could keep in the pocket. C.C. was always here today. I had hope in that car ride home. C.C. had hope that we could be us again. I could be the boy she fell in love with again. She never stopped being the girl I fell in love with. I had a chance then; it was the best chance I would ever have.

We all make poor decisions and "do it dumb," as my dad would say to me when I messed up a pipe solder he taught me. Fact. I turned the water off, but it kept trickling out of the crack I was trying to close with my mess of flux and lead-free solder. "If you can't stop the water, you lose your bond," he told me. How do I stop it? He handed me a piece of white bread. I had no idea what was happening. I think about that day now, about that piece of bread, and I smile. There is nothing more mundane and commonplace on the food pyramid than white bread. We pull it to pieces and feed it to birds; we ball it up into gluten projectiles during food fights. You cannot find a trash can left out on the road without half a moldy loaf of the stuff languishing at the bottom. But for my daughter, that mad dash to empty the bread aisle at the supermarket makes total sense. Every time I see her, which today is an average of two times per week, she asks me to make her a peanut butter and jelly sandwich, sometimes another one for lunch the next day; a mound of peanut butter, spread to the edges of one piece of bread, a thin film of jelly on the other, the same way every time.

Like me, Cleo likes her solitude. She likes to read and game and video-chat with her close group of friends. She is a brilliant artist and works best while free of distractions. She is so much like me when I was young; I like to think she will always honor her privacy, using it as a safe space instead of a devil's playground as I did later in life. Even at eighteen, she emerges from her space, stares up at me with those luminous brown eyes, the ones I fell in love with the first time she opened them, and in her unaffected voice she asks if I can make her a sandwich. And I will make it every time just to spend another moment with her. Such a trifling thing we take for granted every day; for me, it carries the same weight as saying, "I will always be here for you."

Back to our broken pipe . . . Dad pulled a piece from the humble square and shoved it in the pipe so it could soak up the water. The stream of water temporarily staunched; I successfully soldered the pipe. The bread would just dissolve inside, and the water would flow through the bonded copper. Elegant and effective. I thought of this lesson he was teaching me when I first heard a revelation one night in Livengrin: whatever you put before your recovery, or your bond with the life you want, you will lose. My kids just wanted their dad back; C.C., her husband. I wanted to give them all of me before I even had the tools to do it. I kept shoving excuses in the pipe instead of fixing the hole. I had the opportunity and resources to do it. I kept diluting out all my natural "feel good" hormones and emotions in a chemical tide rather than staunching it long enough to do the work I had to do to get right. I had no angel on my shoulder opposing the devil on the other; I had a legion of them around me, who just wanted to see us happy. I realize using too many adverbs just bloats what we are trying to say, but saying this without ambiguity makes me feel like a sociopath. Feel free to omit the qualifier in this next sentence; I cannot. I apparently did not want to see us happy.

Instead of doing what I should have and telling her about that teeny reservation, I let it lie. *No big deal*, I thought—*it will pass.* I would let some time pass, convince her that a drink now and then is no big deal, a trivial treat. Well, I did not do that. In fact, I upped the timetable quite a bit. I had returned to work and the smiles and support of my colleagues. If anyone knew why I was gone, there was no shred of judgment, just genuine joy I was back. After six weeks of my transformative month inside, I had waited long enough. I had no consequences. I still had my career with no caveats, my kids were happy to have me back, and I still had C.C.. Time to fuck it all up again. Her first weekend trip away, I got some vodka and transferred it into water bottles without spilling a drop. I was almost shaking with anticipation at that first drink, the demon inside me writhing with glee. That fuse between the spark and the inevitable boom gets shorter every time we light it. Within a week or so, C.C. woke me up in the guest room one morning. I was lying in a fetal position on top of the bedsheets, fully clothed. I did not look like I peacefully fell asleep watching a movie. Back to shameful groveling and "I'm sorry" and "What can I do?" But there was less regret this time. Remember, in my warped mind, I had not lost anything substantial, trivializing C.C.'s love and trust beneath the weight of a job or status. I was leaking, but I still flowed. Always living her best but preparing for the worst, C.C. put a sobriety contract in place to which I agreed and signed, thinking it would never be necessary. The first stipulation of failure to remain sober was I left and went into a sober house. I made some calls and Sheila, my counselor at Livengrin, got me into one. I moved in that night, slipping my Mr. Fixit back on.

C.C. was still trying to keep our family together by giving me yet another chance. Channeling my powers of deception, C.C. told our innocent children I was in Honduras again for an extended stay while I was a rehab inpatient. She had to lie to our children, gambling that I would do what was right. While my children believed their father was a noble man helping the impoverished, I was squandering the opportunity to be the dad they deserved. Even if the gamble paid off, the little lie lingers forever.

The only two times I get honest are when I am scared enough

or drunk enough. When I was drunk enough, I told my children the truth of where I was. That I was in rehab instead of Honduras, that I was getting better for them. Cleo seemed scared and overwhelmed; Adam seemed confused. But I was telling the truth—that was a good thing, right? Suddenly a trivial white lie told to preserve their image of their father became a monumental deception, especially told though the haze of a drunk in remission from reality. What an asshole. Now they knew that I was sick and would be leaving again because I was still sick. I felt so ashamed. They were the only two people I loved with my life that did not know my dirty little secret.

Independence Lodge is in Levittown, PA, which, on a map, looks like it was kicked to the curb by its older, good-looking cousin, Philadelphia. It is bordered by other blue-collared step-towns in PA and, of course, New Jersey. Much like my recovery dorm in Livengrin, my new home was built on structure, service, and brotherhood. But now, I was getting up every morning and going to work. As before, I met good men trying to be better. In the house I was in, there was a single hall separating the bedrooms from the common rooms. At the end of the hall was a full-length mirror so that every man leaving for the day to go to jobs or meetings or to build a better version of himself would see the words written at the top of it: The Person Most Responsible for Your Recovery. More than once, I thought I saw my dad rounding that corner.

I could relate tales about going through the twelve steps for the first time with my first sponsor or ordering hoagies for the house on my night to cook dinner or the rave-like energy of being in a house of men a decade or more my junior or sober fun in hooka lounges, but the whole experience was just a trivial distraction from what I really wanted. I missed my children. I missed Adam's excited yelping, "My daddy's home, my daddy's home!" when I returned home from Livengrin. I missed my Cleo's sweet smile and her presenting me with a "Welcome Home" poster she and Adam put together. Those massive emotions from their little mouths. I put them in a mental case, like the glass Detolfs I stored my collectibles in—like they would always be there for me to admire.

As Cleo was older, her beautiful mind started to see me differently. During one of my visits, C.C. came home with her, and I could tell by her face something was wrong. Her eyes were red as she said Cleo had something she wanted to tell me. It was autumn, my favorite season, and I loved when our home, sheltered by giant oak and beech trees, became blanketed with a rustic rainbow of fallen leaves. Cleo was outside kicking them in to small piles. I asked her if she had something to tell me. Still making piles, she told me she did not know if she loved me anymore. Small mouth, massive emotion. I asked her why she thought that, and she said she did not know. Trying not to cry, I said that was okay and that I would always love her no matter what. C.C., always trying to preserve my own childlike emotions, said she probably was confusing love with presence, and because I was not there, the love wasn't either, or something to that effect. Children change and grow so quickly. What was so important to them yesterday is barely a memory today. They need their parents to be constant. I was not for her. I was trivializing her growth for my own even as I was telling her and myself I was doing it all for her. Those little lies we tell ourselves. I was hurt by what she said, but after what I put her and her brother and her mother through, I could expect no less. Those little betrayals build up and make a mess when they topple.

I was still in outpatient treatment and met more recovery mates fighting the good fight. One of the women in the group, Cheryl, saw right through me. I was the only one in the group who had not lost their job as a nurse. Wearing my mask of humility, I feigned the same and pretended to relate to the men and women trying to change themselves. Soon, that false modesty would be shredded by fear. A few weeks later, after I lost my second job as a nurse, Cheryl would admit she thought I had not lost enough to "hit bottom," the infamous destination of all tortured souls where we decide to climb back up or dig deeper.

After another six weeks, the amount of time it took me to start drinking again after transitioning from inpatient to out, C.C.'s trust in me had built up enough that she agreed to let me take her out for her birthday. I gave her the anthology I wrote her. I was proud of it. The connecting story was a possible future where C.C., older and gracefully aged, was packing up our house coming upon mementos, small things that triggered memories that became the different, sensationalized tales of the day we met, our wedding day, Cleo and Adam's rescue mission, and a symbolic tale of me as a wounded soldier, surrendering my fight with addiction with C.C. at my side. The connecting arc ended well with us together and happy in a future I truly wanted to see but never would. She called me shortly after I dropped her off, having read the whole thing in a single sitting. I still tear up at her reaction, saying how beautiful and brilliant it was and how much she loved it. Those small words of affirmation she knew I needed to hear. A short stack of forty-two pages that brought her so much joy.

A week later, during my visit home, she said that she needed to talk about something. Of course, I went right to "what did I do?" I was legitimately sober, so I knew that was not the issue. I thought it had to with the logistics of visitation or revising my sobriety contract. We went up to our room, she closed the door, and jumped me. We had not made love as passionate as that since that first incredible summer after we met when our love was new and our lust seismic. "It should always be this way," I said as we collapsed into each other's arms. I kissed her neck; it was salty with sweat. I meant that. I wanted that. Everything was going to be okay. Color filled my white knuckles.

We descended the stairs in love again. I had a twelve-step meeting to get to before curfew. I kissed my kids goodbye. Their beautiful faces. I gave C.C. a tender kiss at the door. Her facial muscles could not betray her joy, her almond eyes squinting, her full lips stretched wide. The moldy "bread" of betrayal, deceit, and broken promises dissolved in an instant and the tide of love that brought us this far gushed. I felt amazing. But as good as I ever feel, I want to feel better.

9

DESPERATION GIGS

"Fuck, fuck, fuck," hissed Dave through clenched teeth, "and fuck these fucked-up cul-de-sacs with no fucking address-es." Dave was a delivery driver for a pizza joint in Bristol, PA, a limbo between the gentrified suburbs of Philly and the conurbation of trap houses and recovery havens of Levittown, which had a thirty-minutes-or-it's-free delivery policy. Dave is the reason this particular purveyor of pan pizza, once a childhood royal delicacy, marched out in an iron pan as hot as the sun and laid with reverence a foot from you just as your jukebox banger finally spun up, no longer has that policy. This was Dave's third post-thirty-minute delivery this week and he was stressed. His eyes darted from one cookie-cutter condo to the next, praying for an address that matched the one scrawled on his rapidly cooling passenger pizzas. A magnetic restaurant logo crowning his Impreza, its signature spoiler sold long ago, leaned into the parabola of his fourth cul-de-sac turn-in. Then the muted thud of hitting something with your car. Dave screeched to a halt. "What. The. Fuck." The driver door creaked open. Dave crept out with the reluctant horror of a child called by his full name. Each step to the front of the car took an eon. Just before he reached the front of his car, he heard a weak "Meow." Feeling sick, he rounded the hood and saw a mangy tabby cat lying in a bed of leaves molded into the gutter. "Oh my God. Oh fuck, I'm sorry, kitty." His eyes welled with tears. Dave used to have a cat until, in a heroin-induced oblivion, he collapsed on it. While Dave snored and survived, "Purrito" wriggled and writhed and went to Kitty Heaven. Now, Dave had just mortally wounded another cat. Purrito's protracted death was traumatizing to Dave. For weeks, he had nightmares of his cat suffocating under him.

He would not see another cat suffer.

Dave walked closer to the tabby; there was no blood that he could see, but it was missing a leg. He made a retching sob. "No, no, no, I'm so sorry," he whimpered. Dave slowed his shuddering. "Okay, kitty, I'm gonna make this right." He walked till he stood right over the ailing cat. It just looked up at him, its little mouth "meowing." Dave raised up his leg, leveling his boot over the cat's head. "You rest now, little guy. No more pain," he said, stifling a sob, then he brought his boot down with a practiced skinhead stomp, crushing the kitty's skull with a wet crack. Dave let out a shuddering breath and looked to the sky for redemption.

"Oh my God!" wailed a woman, running toward Dave. "What did you do?"

"Uh, is this your cat? I'm so sorry. I hit it with my car—" Dave stammered.

"You killed her! You cocksucker! This is bestiality," the woman roared.

"I . . . don't think that's bestiality."

"Don't you deny it. I saw you . . . Cindy Clawford . . ." She winced, remembering Dave curb-stomp her cat. "I'm calling the police."

The woman stormed off.

"No, ma'am. Please. I'm sorry," Dave pleaded. Remembering

what he was doing there in the first place, he held up the greasy, crumpled receipt from the pizzas. "Do you know where this is?"

A surprisingly short time later, a police officer rolled up with all the excitement you would expect from a 911 call reporting a murdered cat.

"He killed my Cindy," she cried.

"Lady, I put him out of his misery. He was missing a leg," Dave pleaded his case.

"She only had three legs!"

Dave was confused.

The cop made a sweep of the crime scene and stopped at the passenger side, crouching near the wheel well. Pushing up his mirrored aviators, he motioned Dave over to his position.

"You said you hit something?" asked the cop.

Dave pointed to the late Cindy Clawford. "Yeah, the cat in the —" Dave followed the cop's pointing finger to a freshly mangled raccoon twisted around his tire.

BACK IN THE kitchen of the pizza place, where all the magic happens, Vinny and I laughed so hard we cried as Dave finished his harrowing tale, though the tears were likely from the caustic gas liberated from the remnants of wing sauce we were scrubbing from the mixing bowls. Dave told us to stop being douchebags and that he thought he was doing the right thing. Dave was a recovering addict like me. He was still regaining his humanity and sense of self and still emotionally fragile in early sobriety. The fabled pan pizzas inched along their conveyor belt oven. I told him sometimes we "do it dumb" but it does not make us dumb. I was slinging aphorisms and one-liner life quotes with acumen these days. "Desperation Gigs," or "D-Gigs," the jobs I took between the involuntary sabbaticals of my career as a nurse, always gave me perspective.

Oh, right. I am sorry for jumping ahead again. As an anachronist, old habits die hard. The last time we saw our antagonist, me, of course, I was a respectable anesthetist and leaving my beautiful family, the very thing I claimed to stay sober for and counted on to keep me sober, to go to a twelve-step meeting with my housemates. I went to that meeting, but I made a stop at a liquor store first.

Yep.

Except now I bought some energy drinks to mix with it. My time with millennials was rubbing off on me. I drank half the can of one and filled it back up with vodka, then drank that back down on the way to the meeting. At least I never went to an AA meeting drunk. Until I did. I got away with it that night even though a few days later, after that ever-shortening fuse sizzled to the "boom," Jack, an old friend from Livengrin who followed a similar post-rehab relapse path to the same house, told me he smelled the booze on me. He said he wished he'd have pulled me aside that night to crush it before it got worse. I wished he did too. But it would not have mattered. By then, the gravity I was exuding was too great. I would have to hit something pretty hard to break the fall.

I got away it with two days later when I met C.C., Cleo, and Adam at the mall to see a movie, even though C.C. suspected something was off. Two days after that, after my two tiny "victories," it was time to take this show on the road. My employer was gracious enough to give me an additional month after my month in Livengrin without twenty-four-hour call shifts. This was my first call shift back since that furlough. Now, with my mind as rational as it has probably ever been, it is difficult to describe what was going through my head that night as I brought a bottle of vodka to my call room.

AA tells us the alcoholic has no defense against the first drink. "Drink" here is metaphorical. A relapse back to our vice is about as sudden as growing grass if we were ever in recovery. The path back to ruin starts with "I," as Charlie cautioned, but we cannot discount our environment. Speaking for my profession, the rigors of caring for human lives, from saving someone's life on the OR table to watching children die, will chip away at our resolve. Even the most stout, joyful healthcare practitioner has their exemplary bedside manner whittled away after years in practice. For me, long hours were a trigger. Working a twenty-four-hour shift once per week where, often, I was carefully managing potentially deadly anesthetics and patient vital signs for the duration became a terrible grind—at least that was what I kept telling myself. Compartmentalization is a skill we nurses learn early in our practice, a necessity to wall off some of the horrific things we see. We say we become desensitized to the suffering and trauma and the lateral violence, the phenomenon of directing our inward dissatisfaction toward each other and ourselves, but we never do. Hearing coworkers look forward to a drink after a stressful shift was as common as saying STAT. That day, I did not want to wait till after my shift.

I knew I had to get back in the OR, but I had some downtime so I took a few shots in my room. No big deal. Some breath mints as a backup because vodka had no scent and back to the OR I went. Whenever we stop using, our addictive mind freezes in place, waiting with the endless patience of, well, a nurse. That part of ourselves remembers the standard ration of shots, pills, or lines we did to get where we wanted to be. When we finally thaw it out, our addiction is ready to pick up right where we left off. Our bodies, having repaired the physiological damage and rebalanced our reward centers, are not ready. After leaving my room, the next thing I remember, I was sitting in our lounge with one of the anesthesiologists, or "ologists," as we referred to them out of brevity and to distinguish their status among we lesser nurses, regarding me with concern. Martin said I looked like I had been drinking and had "nystagmus," doctor speak for crossed eyes. My damn lazy eye always did wander when I was hammered. The worst thing about a blackout is the dawning horror that you do not know what to apologize for or what lies to spin to explain actions of which you have no memory. Paudric, another ologist and friend of mine, burst into the room in plain clothes. He was on his way home when another friend tipped him off about me and came straight back. He gave me that "let's get you the fuck out of here" look but Martin protested saying security was on the way to take me to the ER for a tox screen. Paudric wanted to speak with me alone and then other docs showed up to escort him out. I would have jumped out the window hand in hand with him if I could, but I was too petrified to do anything but sit there silently. Paudric was yelling at Martin, saying this was contained until he called security. Now the hospital was involved. Now I was fucked.

All I know for certain is that the patient under my care was not harmed in any way. Mercifully, another anesthetist arrived to relieve me as scheduled. When she did arrive, she realized something was off. She did what she should have by calling Martin, then watched me stumble down the hall. Back in the lounge, more staff were arriving to, as it seemed to me, block my exit. Not that I could run in a straight line anyway. I had the vague sensation of falling. As drunk as I was, I rummaged around for my Mr. Fixit mask, which was just my sputtering fight or flight response. As slow as my reaction time was, my damage control center was running through possible consequences at lightning speed. What concerned me most was what to tell C.C., followed closely by how I would keep my job. My blood test in the ER showed a blood alcohol level more than twice the limit allowed to operate a motor vehicle, let alone care for another person who trusted me to render them the most vulnerable they have ever been. What would I tell C.C.? We'd spoken just a few hours ago, her voice intoned with love and the anticipation that I would be back home soon.

I should have been on my way to prison; instead, I was being sequestered in the ER for the night. Paudric convinced the ER attending to ignore the tox screen, saying it was done without the proper chain of consent or some other bullshit. He got them to agree to let me spend the night and repeat a breathalyzer in the morning. I had six hours to blow negative. It would not be enough time. What is it in me that makes a good woman sacrifice her own sanity, a good man jeopardize his career just to keep me from going down? What is it in me that spits in the face of such grace? Once, years after my actions in addiction first started raining consequences down on C.C. and me, when there was doubt I could even work as an anesthetist after spending years and our resources on education, I said to her she would be better off with me dead. That was part drama but also part pragmatism; I had a sizable life insurance policy she could cash in on. As I felt like a breathing burden to her, that was my way of "doing the right thing." This upset her, of course, but she understood what I meant. She was beginning to understand the darkness inside me. She feared it, but she stayed by my side, thinking she, and our sweet Cleo and Adam, growing in her womb, would be enough to pull me out. It seems such a small ask in the face of all we had. Just be good. Just be me. I wanted to tear this fucking thing out of me and curb-stomp it like Dave. I had to talk to her, to hear her voice, to break her heart, again, sooner rather than later. I cannot remember what I said, but she understood. Her response was not in complete sentences. All I remember her saying was she had to go.

I was woken up at 5:00 a.m. and given the test. My mouth tasted like something died in it, likely my career. A big breath in and a long blow though a straw, the breathalyzer singing with my breath. I thought for a moment I would get away with it one more time. But numbers tell no lies. An unforgiving ".05" flashed on the machine. Technically, I could drive, but they did not let me.

For the second time, I was escorted out of the hospital and put into a cab; it would not be the last.

I had the cab let me off at a bus stop and rode back to the hospital to get my car. On the way, my sponsor called to let me know, considering my continued sobriety, he and the house managers agreed I could move into the "big boy" house in neighboring Bristol, with my own room, and start adopting some managerial duties. Is that irony? I never know how to use that word in the proper context. Cosmic joke seemed more appropriate. I dropped my news and got put into a different house. I was given twenty-four hours to report myself to the Board of Nursing before the hospital made their formal complaint. What choice did I have? None if I wanted a chance to work as a nurse again. Did I? This was that moment when I could have looked at an emerging pattern of a career choice that had led me to self-medicate twice under the extreme stress of it. But that was bullshit. I was a self-sabotaging, untreated addict with a short list of other mental disorders that happened to implode while working in an admirable field. Unless I wanted to figure out what I wanted to be when I grow up again, and C.C. would have supported me in this, there was no other choice. That boundless imagination I had when I was younger waned. I just wanted to make enough money to pursue what I wanted to do in life, which up to that point did not amount to much more than continuing to chase that fabled euphoria through alcohol and any other substance that took me out of myself. I would be making less money now as I was called back into the hospital to be terminated later that day.

A few days later, C.C. agreed to see me. She was sitting on the bed in our guest room, looking out the window. Andrew Wyeth could not have painted a more evocative scene. Her pretty face was tired. She gave me an ultimatum, her first despite all I had already put her through: get this done or we are done, was the gist. When I first went to Livengrin, C.C. did not see the egoistic self-saboteur. She saw her husband, who she loved and believed was sicker than she ever realized. Even when I was scared and frustrated after leaving home to go to Independence Lodge, she reassured me, saying I needed this to get well "and then you'll come back to me." I still remember the love in her voice, almost nostalgic for when we were us. Now her tone was all business. She was beginning to see me for the bad investment I was. I left relieved. If I had her, everything would be okay, I could make this right, but things were never the same between us again.

Ever since her decision to go through with our marriage, I placed C.C. on a pedestal, like a goddess to worship for the life she had given me. With every absolution she gave for my sins, that pedestal soon rose to a tower. Like in any hierarchy, the ones on the lower tiers get resentful. I was no exception. In her final letter to me, she debunked my claim that I thought she was above me, citing that it was another fiction I created to justify my shame of never living up to her imagined expectations of me, further justifying my will to do what I wanted. She is probably right— she usually is when it comes to me—but I put her up there as a benchmark, a place and a person to aspire to and eventually reach; it was my own failing that came to resent the peak I created.

Delivering pizzas was my current weekend D-Gig and ranked low on my list of favorites, historically. My favorite, until it was not, as I mentioned previously, was working as a personal trainer, or "FitPro," as we were lauded, but more on that later. My first official gigs kicked off more than a decade prior, working as a unit secretary in the same hospital where I lost my first nursing job, supplemented with working with my brother-in-law who was a contractor, repairing roofs, installing decks, and other ball-breaking work. I was grateful for the opportunities. Not only did my first employer not press charges against me, but they also continued to provide me with a living. Jimmy, C.C.'s brother, could barely afford to pay me but kept me on through the entire summer. Watching his hands, scarred and calloused from years of labor, work evoked fond memories of my father. Going to work with him on occasion and watching him work around our home was the closest we got to quality time. Only a few years older, Jimmy felt more like a father figure than a brother. He struggled with life as well, but he did what he had to and ground through.

I felt I earned my pay, but I began to resent the underlayment of charity beneath these acts of kindness as my ego grew back and entitlement set in. My unit clerk position was a walk of shame, seeing former coworkers, including my former supervisor who had my early discontent with the profession pegged from the start. She would regard me with a knowing grin. I got what I deserved. As fun as it could be helping Jimmy, playing with miter saws, nail guns, electric grinders, and other "man" shit, I just felt like a grunt. Enormous acts of faith that meant little to me in the long game.

After a weekend of driving through neighborhoods I learned to fear as a kid and getting stiffed on tips, from Monday to Friday I worked at a factory fabricating cosmetics.

Yup.

These were jobs I did not want to get me out of a house I did not want to be in, but I earned my way into both. It should have been a learning experience, but I spent most of my time measuring shimmering shades of sand, weighing buckets of binding oil, cleaning up all the excess, then leaving to sling pizzas and wash wing bowls falling deeper into a shame hole. Guys in the house got me hooked up with both jobs. In the Lodge, there was a grizzled elegance in the way we all healed. We were all broken in some way and knew it was easier to fix each other than fix ourselves. Make no mistake, for many who worked at these institutions, it was a living. And no doubt they managed their lives better than I have with a fraction of my former income. You cannot be overqualified for a job if you do not have one. I could have spent time retooling my resume, maybe look for something more in line with my education, but I kept looking for the familiar path back to where I was. The easier, softer way. But no matter how many figures I made, it would never be enough. That hole in the pipe was still wide open.

I met people who were decades of life above and below me and had their lives together. Vinny, my fellow pizza boy, nineteen, was banking cash before going into the Air Force academy the following year. Petra, the woman who hired me at the pizza joint, had a history of addiction as well. She shared her story with me and how she found a way to live again and support her two children. She was a big Nolan Batman fan, and her favorite quote was, "It is not how many times we fall, but how many times we get back up." Chandra had worked at the cosmetic factory for thirty years and treated everyone there, from lifers to D-Giggers like me, like family. That Christmas, she brought in a tin of shortbread cookies for each member of the staff. Even if she did roll in a Benz to the blighted lot and saunter into the factory in a fur coat—I never figured that out—it was still very generous; she was just a good person and wanted to share her joy with every life she touched. All the guys in the house walked toward that mirror proud of what they saw, despite the mistakes they'd made. They were all walking, talking lessons on how to live. They had problems like anyone else, some the same problems as me, but they were getting through it. I kept trying to go around it.

All those little gigs taught me a lot about what it meant to be human, let alone be a man. They also netted me a few pieces of sage advice: assume your delivered pizza has toppings on it you did not order, and for any of you who wear makeup, if you knew the kind of hands that fondled the constituent parts of your nude lipstick or matte eyeshadow, you would go au naturel. But like all the saw dust I kicked up helping Jimmy build his decks or the shimmery sand I weighed out every day, I let those lessons pour through my fingers focusing only on how I must have been the only one alive to start rehab with a successful career and dream home and work my way back to high school occupations and nine roommates. Nowhere to go but up, right? Remember, I am the roller coaster, and this was just the trick hill. Get your hands up for the big drop.

It was Christmas Eve, and with an inability to imbibe, I was bingeing on the next best thing—my mom's from-scratch chocolate chip cookies. I've enjoyed them since I was a kid, the same recipe, sugar, both white and brown, flour, eggs, and walnuts all in a one-bite package. After I left home, when I visited for the holiday, she would always fill one of those tins that held that crappy, tri-flavor popcorn to the top with cookies for me to take. I had my yearly tin open at my feet and I was eating my cookies like an addict as C.C. and I sat with my mom. C.C. and her always got along, but their relationship had gone from one of adoration to slightly adversarial after C.C. drove me to Livengrin. C.C. watched me with concern as I watched the clock. It had been six weeks since C.C.'s clock started ticking in the guest room. Six weeks after I got out of inpatient treatment, I relapsed and left home. Six weeks in the recovery house, I relapsed and lost my career. Had I researched it or recalled the lectures from rehab or discussions with my sponsor on the refractory period of the obsession and compulsion of addiction, I would have known that window of time was critical in early recovery. If I could just get over that hump, life would get better.

But all I could think about was that, in three days, I would climb back into the lion's den of the Board monitoring program, and all I could see was a life without another drink. I hated what I was thinking; I hated myself for thinking it. After saying goodbye to C.C., Cleo, and Adam, I would drive my mom to my aunt's for our traditional Christmas Eve dinner, still watching that clock. I would see my family and I would enjoy their company. I would see sad eyes brighten when they saw how good I looked, how strong I was. Those little words of affirmation I needed so much were just noise that night. I drove my mother back home way too fast—she told as much—thanked her for the cookies, and gave a terse goodbye. In the car, I checked my phone; I had fifteen minutes. I did not think I would make it; a small part of me was relieved. Traffic cops apparently had better things to do on the Eve of Baby Jesus's arrival as I drove like a demon in the drizzle without detection and walked through the auto doors of the liquor store already disabled for closing. I grabbed the first bottle of vodka I could find and left, the doors locking behind me. If I was a Jedi, I would have heard dozens of voices, give or take, crying out in anger and disbelief.

Go ahead, ask it. Everyone else has. What the fuck is wrong with me? Many diagnoses, professional opinions, and personality profiles have been rendered, and friends and family have weighed in on everything from me as overly stressed to just an asshole. They are probably all right, but none of it matters. The twelve steps, or any system of recovery, is a "simple program for complicated people." Even someone as constitutionally incapable of being honest with themselves and in deep denial of their flaws as I was can recover if we truly want to. Every relapse starts with "I stopped." I stopped going to meetings. I stopped talking to my sponsor. I stopped playing the tape. I stopped giving a shit. Many have it much worse than me but thrive in a life beyond their wildest dreams because they got out of their own way.

If anyone smelled the booze on me at the Lodge that night, they did not say anything or hoped I could not be that stupid. As JC's B-day this year was with C.C.'s family, given the circumstances, I drank another third of the fifth and went to my mom's house for another family tradition. It is not insanity if it is practice. A few days later, after the roller coaster hit its terminal depth, she said she thought she smelled the booze. The day after Christmas, two thousand years ago, Jesus, Mary, and Joseph chilled in the manger, enjoying some of the only quiet moments they would have as a family, not realizing the ripple their lives would make on the world. Two thousand years later, I did not realize the ripples the actions I took that day would make on my family. Well, I did, but only if I got caught. Of course, I did.

I figured out pizza delivery is more fun with a buzz on. I sipped that last third of my bottle of vodka in between deliveries and was having a blast; so much so, I blacked out in the AA meeting where I met my housemates after. My memory rebooted with my sponsor staring at me after the serenity prayer commencement, telling me I was drunk. "Nah," I said. "A little," he said. He gave that look your mom or dad would give when you did something wrong, but they blamed themselves. John was my sponsor and swore by continuance, staying with a sponsee after taking him through the twelve steps. The kind of bond you form with a sponsor is almost symbiotic. He did not blame himself for what I did but he felt my pain and shame. But he knew better than to let my insanity infect him.

That was three strikes, if you count my failing that got me into IL. Brian King, the owner and operator of Independence Lodge, recruited heavily from Livengrin and other local body brokers. He knew about me and how I fucked up after Livengrin. Now I fucked up on his turf. Twice. He specializes in lost causes, and he said he would let me stay in his house if I went to a detox unit first.

Nope.

So, now I got kicked out of the house I went to after I was kicked out of the house I went to after I was kicked out of my home. This Russian doll of recovery houses would be adorable if it were not so pathetic. As I packed up my car that morning, some of the men asked what I would do. I did not know. I felt a terrible emptiness and shame so deep I just wanted to drive to the ocean and keep driving. That familiar weight of abandonment and resentment pressed on me. I just kept moving. I had a scheduled visit to see my children that day, a supervised visit with C.C.'s mom as the monitor. I adjusted my dad mask as best I could, but my mind was racing in circles. What the fuck was I going to do?

At the end of the visit, I kissed my children goodbye; it felt like I would never see them again. I was on the road when I got the call. It was C.C.. She asked where I was. Her voice was tinged with the disbelief it had the night I was chained in the ER, praying for my lungs to outsmart zero order kinetics, but she was seething. I knew the ripple of my choice would bounce back on me but what hurt the most was how she found out.

When C.C. and I were still together and happy-ish, Adam used to run into my car looking for loose change to put in his blue piggy bank. That day, I was in Cleo's room talking with her when he ran out for a score. What he saw confused him. In my car, piled high with bags and loose clothes, he could not find any change. He did not know what someone on the run looked like, but there must have been a visceral fear in him that something was not right. Life is the rise of consciousness but also the reduction of input. When we are young, we lack the filters we put in place to blot out the terrors of the world. My bug-out bags, spilling onto the seats, chipped a bit of Adam's innocence away, just as mine was all those years ago finding my dad in a place I hoped he was not.

All those little deceits and horrors matter. Even today, years later, when my baby boy, now practically a man, gets in my car and sees a bag or a pile of loose gym clothes I was too lazy to vacate, I see him pause just for a microsecond. A splinter of fear in his handsome face remembering a day steeped in fear and doubt. *Oh. My. God.* I did that to him. He asked his grandmom about it. She took one look and knew exactly what happened. As I kissed my kids goodbye, she did not say anything. She had her mask on too.

C.C. checked in with Brian at Independence Lodge and confirmed what she was waiting for. On the phone with me, she did all the talking. I only remember three words. She said it like a movie line, like she had been practicing it for weeks but not sure how it would sound on camera, flooded with lights and emotion.

"I'm leaving you." Cut. That's a wrap. At least I never threw away the best thing that ever happened to me, until I did. The rest of that day is a blur, and not because I was drunk; the empty vodka bottle was still in my car. The only other thing I remember is the desperate plea I made via text: *Please don't leave me. Stay with me, love. Just one more time.*

10

STAND-IN SAVIORS

April held my hand as we walked up the carpeted aisle toward the stage where Pastor Joe, donned in jeans and a Hawaiian shirt, St. James Bible in hand, presided. Through all the fear, shame, guilt, and humiliation, I kept hearing one word: *surrender*. Calvary Chapel Church (CCC) looked like a new-age auditorium, bereft of the requisite stained-glass windows, painted murals, and stench of incense of the churches I frequented as a Catholic schoolboy. Gospel rock filled the hall as a full band jammed onstage. I waded into a crowd of other broken souls, holding their surrogates' hands as we huddled up to the curve of the stage like sperm against an egg. April squeezed my hand tighter. I was crying. She looked at me, nodding, and saying "surrender" over and over, waiting for her gentle commands to punch a hole into what felt like a higher perception, its purifying light washing away my fear and shame as it did for her years ago.

I have known a few born-again Christians with varying degrees of indoctrination, from spiritually awakened to zealot. Most I knew were Bible-thumpers who were quick to judge your sins to drown out their own. Raised in the dogma of the Catholic Church, there was an inherent prejudice against any other faith that was not ours. But just as experience and an open mind bring greater understanding and tolerance of other races and cultures, pain and desperation opened my mind to anything that would take it away. I never liked going to Mass until after I came to terms with my addiction, suddenly finding meaning in the gospel readings. A Big Book of excerpts works much the same way a good sermon does—it gives what you need when you need it. When the pupil is ready, the teacher appears, or when the addict is desperate, signs of salvation appear on faded billboards, the gospel speaks to you as if it knew your thoughts, someone in a meeting says exactly what you needed to hear; fucking fortune cookie scrolls seem to have the secret to life in their sugary shell.

Whether we believe there is or is not a Supreme Being guiding our destiny, the stories and teachings in the Holy Bible or the Koran or any other religious tome are reminders on how to live right. But as with all signs of a higher purpose working in my life, those meanings waned as I gradually got my old life back. April was one of my "stand-in saviors," a host of discarded angels in my life who gave me inspiration, hope, and, when needed, a kick in the ass. They helped me to get out of myself and held up the mirror I never wanted to see. Of course, C.C. did all these things and more, but on my steady course of upending our life every few years, understudies in her role were essential. Coworkers, counselors, friends old and new, father figures, one-night-stand speakers at meetings—all fundamental to my ascension as a whole person and ultimately discarded as I got back to my life and C.C. headlined again. I keep pieces of them with me; every lesson in this memory dump was informed through the acts of kindness from people that owed me nothing yet gave everything of themselves.

April was a fellow anesthetist at my previous job. When I first returned to work after my inpatient stay, she came up to me, gave a hug, and with tears in her eyes said, "I am so glad you are here." I did not know her well, but that gracious show of emotion told me we had been through the same thing. Each day, she asked if I would say a small prayer with her in the hall to the OR. I felt a bit embarrassed, and waited for an eventual pitch about her church, but I obliged. In an environment like ours, where it is necessary to compartmentalize stress and blunt emotion, vulnerability is rare and impactful. She always carried around a Bible in a zip case. In the years I knew her, I always saw her reading it on breaks. There were Post-it Notes, filled with her writing, between almost every page. Most people scoffed at her "addiction" to faith, but I often wished I could believe that strongly in something.

Pastor Joe spread his arms over us. "Hold your heads high. You have looked down for too long. Give your will to God and let him do the rest." It felt like I was breaking a commandment but, in that place, with ears filled with guitar, bass, and drums instead of an organ, I felt relief. Not every member of CCC was an addict, but there were enough that recovery meetings were held in the bowels of the church twice per week with Pastor Tim. The "street preacher," as he was known, used Bible pages as rolling papers; he said he only pulled from the New Testament, though. He turned every meeting into a thundering sermon. He was one of my favorite stand-ins. The church also sponsored a recovery house for those in need. If I was as quick to reach out for help before I needed it as I was when I was drowning in desperation, my life would look much different.

The day after my "shove death" of my life when C.C. had finally had enough, I was back at my mom's house. Saint Peg, the greatest savior of all, she never gave up on anyone, least of all me. April kept in touch and, like all my saviors, she answered prayers I had not yet made. She reached out that day and asked to meet for dinner. I had just eaten but I went anyway. I confessed my sins and April put me in touch with another savior, Elvin, the Calvary recovery house manager. Two days later, my mom kissed me at her door and gave me one of those Alex and Ani bracelets with a medal of Maximillian Kobe, the patron saint of lost causes, on it. I rarely saw my mom cry, but that day she had tears in her eyes, and I wondered how many unnecessary tears she shed because of me. I thanked her for everything and continued my necessary journey.

C.C. did not file for divorce. Sometime later, when I made my amends to her as part of my ninth step, she told me she was in the lawyer's office but could not go through with it. If someone as good and as pure as she is would stay with me through all the abuse she endured, there must be some ember of good in me, some spark she thought she could fan into the flame we once shared. She made me believe I was the man she deserved. But right now, I was on thin fucking ice. But C.C. was committed. She saw my new house, met Elvin and the other men in there, and went to the weekly meetings with me. Days turned into weeks and weeks into months. I started looking into the mirror again. My dad was there, but so was I, my mask fading into a face I was starting to like.

Our first night out as a couple again was at a friend's wedding. Most of the congregation were my former coworkers. Often, it is others that see change in you before you feel it yourself, and though I was getting plenty of external validation, those giant little words of encouragement, I was feeling it too. Not too long ago, I could not imagine going to a wedding and not drinking; that was my main motivation for being there. With C.C. at my side and a legion of friends smiling and happy to see me alive and well, I started to glimpse the real possibility of a sober and happy life. I was even offered a position with my old employer in one of their pain offices as a technician, assisting with steroid injections for chronic pain, which I accepted. If you stay clean from whatever ails you, life will get better. Mine was getting better, but it had taken a proverbial village to get me this far. Though we must make the choice to change and do the work, we cannot do it without help. C.C.'s aunt Pat and uncle Paul had been in recovery from alcoholism for decades before I met them. Being from the biggest small town on the planet, Philadelphia, Pat knew my aunt who was also an alcoholic back in her glory days. As I became a part of C.C.'s family, I became close with Pat and Paul who eventually learned of my father's battle and eventual death from alcoholism. Being the only two members of a family that liked to imbibe at gatherings who did not drink, they were usually on the outskirts of parties but always felt a kinship with me. More than once, they said I was playing a dangerous game continuing to drink, especially after my addiction to pills became public. I did all I could to avoid them because they were killing my buzz and because, inside, I knew they were right. After Livengrin, Paul reached out to me and stayed in regular contact. After I was kicked out of Independence Lodge, he offered to be my sponsor. Because of his choices in active alcoholism, Paul had a complicated relationship with his only son, and where I saw my next surrogate father, he saw the son he lost.

I knew the only way this truly works is if it is for me, and I saw a life where I wanted to be sober if it gave me back the joy on C.C.'s face, the giddiness in her laugh. I missed the excitement she had to see our children after we went away on a trip together. She literally trembled walking up to our home. I felt so good to be a part of that, a part of her. To be included in her success. "So happy for us," she would correct me when I said I was happy for her as she rose in her career. There was always a dark part of me scoffing at the notion I could be a part of something truly good, always a slave to that foreboding joy, but I saw beyond that now. Perhaps it was Pastor Joe's sermons every Sunday, reading from the actual Bible rather than the cherry-picked, annotated selections from the Catholic Church missals. Or being truly sober in body for more than six months, the longest I had been since I had my first drink as a teenager. I was finally letting all that unconditional love in. I wanted to be back home to be with my children again, to make up for lost time, to make up for my negligence as a father. I would cry in bed at night, thinking about Adam's gentle pleading to play with him when I was too busy drinking or occupied with my own shit to do so. I wanted Cleo to ask me thirty minutes of questions at bedtime until she got so tired, she fell asleep. I began to cut that short so I could get more "me" time having a few more drinks and playing my games or watching my movies. I listened to voicemails I had saved from more than a year ago from C.C. when the love in her voice was undiminished by my bullshit. Nothing is trivial, especially the things we think are.

There was plenty I wanted to stay sober for, but I had only one absolute reason: the random drug screening through the Board of Nursing was unforgiving. One positive screen and my temporary stay of suspension was vacated, leaving a full suspension of three years without appeal. I relied on this more than I wanted to admit but when it comes to saving your life, pride is inconsequential. I am self-efficacious enough to rely on it still as my career as an anesthetist depends on it. I wanted to want to be sober but then, though I never admitted it, fear was my biggest motivator. Dina, my case manager from the Board of Nursing's advocacy and monitoring program, was another "stand-in" who already had me on file as a risk from my initial fall fifteen years ago but gave me another chance. I would not be where I am today without her. I have known Dina for more than seven years now and she has quietly been one of the greatest champions of my sobriety. She has been with me through some of the most difficult legs of this journey and I am proud to say is still in my life. People will care about us if we let them. Contradictory to my view of the world, most of it wants to see us succeed.

At nine months of sobriety, nine months away from my home, I was welcomed backed to it. I will never forget Adam's declaration of "Finally" during a family meeting discussing my return. It was our biggest challenge as a family, but we were all in together

—no more secrets. Of course, I still tried to keep some of my own. You did not think I would come out of another extended rehab experience without another bad habit, did you? In the Calvary house, I learned about growth hormone peptides, a burgeoning performance enhancement drug (PED) that was said to be the fountain of youth and virtually undetectable on standard urine screens. Steroids and PEDs are a common bedfellow to an addict's more recreational vices. Beyond protein, creatine, and over-the-counter workout stimulants, I had never used anything like these peptides, and though being in the middle of a drug monitoring program and, well, being me put starting a new regimen of supplements that were only administered through subcutaneous injection with a needle in the bad decision bin, I still needed my something. Of course, C.C. found them and the needle. She stabbed me in the chest with it when she confronted me.

"You like to keep things interesting, don't you?" said Dana, our family counselor through Livengrin, whom we still saw each month. While this was not technically a relapse, it was another betrayal of C.C.'s trust. Putting this in terms of dance moves, for years, I was doing the "running man"; over the last year or so, I was doing whatever dance requires you to take two steps forward and one back. Right now, I was moonwalking. Dana was another savior, and she likely saved my marriage that day. C.C. was a communicator. It is what she has done for her entire professional and personal life. Honest communication is what she wanted most from me in our relationship. She believed in the strength of a mediator to facilitate this. Her commitment to us and her faith in me to finally be the man I promised to be was so strong, she was willing to do whatever was left to make us whole. Then, I think she believed the night was darkest before the dawn. It was still very dark, but my eyes had gotten used to it.

C.C. set up meetings with many counselors and counselor couples in our marriage, all good people that gave us good advice.

I marveled at her ingenuity. C.C. had the idea to book a night at a diamond-in-the-rough spa in the Poconos, which was really a thinly veiled counseling session. I was amenable. The couple was renowned in the Kripalu, take-a-swim-in-the-lake crowd. With distinguished gray streaks, they were mere faded copies of their professional photo taken a decade previous, but they were good people. We sauntered around in bathrobes through activities like yoga, flower arranging, and power-napping by day and meeting with the counselor couple by night. They had plenty of good things to say about us and gave good advice, but all I remember was the husband telling me I did not have a relationship problem, "you have a 'you' problem," pointing at me so there was no uncertainty who he was talking about. He was not wrong, but at the time, that was as enlightening to me as Charlie at Livengrin, my grizzled recovery war vet savior, telling me the only thing I had to change about myself was everything. The most influential couple we met was at an idyllic log cabin in Durango, Colorado, hours away from the tourist veneer of cites like Denver and Aspen. There are actual steel yellow signs placed along the winding country roads warning oncoming drivers of cowboy crossings, with a graphic of a dude with a cowboy hat riding a horse. The town is imbued with the remnants of Native American culture with Mesa Verde, a national park, preserving ornate dwellings carved into the sides of mountains by various tribes, its main attraction. Surrounded by snowcapped mountains, amid a fondant of unblemished snow, C.C. and I made the biggest inroads to our relationship since we met. We spent our days in a legit log cabin with horses frolicking in the yard and our nights in a rustic bed-and-breakfast. I found the courage to say things to her I never could, and she listened and vowed to put up with my bullshit. It was her most selfless act in a long history of selfless acts for me. We fell so in love with this near-Nirvana we talked about retiring there together. Another spiritual experience. Two more discarded angels.

Life got back that "new normal" we mused over on our drive home from Livengrin more than a year prior. I stayed clean and things continued to get better. I was still going to meetings and getting drug tested and still thinking about drinking, but I was talking about it. That was something I never used to do because it meant then I could not do it. Baby steps. I was still in counseling through Livengrin with Babette. Ah, Babette, another savior who has been with me since the beginning of the Second Age, what I refer to as my time from Livengrin up to the Third Age, otherwise known as the "endgame," which we will get to. We are still in close contact, and I learned recently she is finally retiring from her career as a drug and alcohol counselor. I asked her how it felt to have saved so many souls. Her answer surprised me. "Heavy," she said. People like Babette put so much of themselves into helping others, they lose a bit of themselves with each effort. I could relate, but my compartmentalization was still fully functioning. She said a lifetime of healing everyone else takes a lot out of you and I wondered how much I had taken from all my angels and how much of it I discarded. I thanked her for the millionth time for all she has done for me. She smiled with all her face and gave me a hug.

With the summer of 2016 approaching, with permission from the Board of Nursing, I began the process of getting back to work as an anesthetist. My former employers, though they liked me and appreciated the work I did for them, were not willing to bring me back into the fold. That stung, but I understood. Besides the obvious drawbridge I burned, there were still many other smaller bridges left in good condition. I was well liked there by many, including some colleagues who had left to work for other practices. When I was granted my first job as an anesthetist, I came with the baggage of a suspended nursing license and history of addiction. I was extremely grateful for the position, the improbable circumstances under which I was hired, notwithstanding. Of course, we know where that gratitude eventually went. If my life was a series of graphs, my inverse relationship with gratitude versus resentment would be the highlight of the portfolio. A former colleague suggested I reach out to another former colleague who had moved on to another practice. He made some calls, and within a week, I had a preliminary offer of employment, baggage and all. I could not believe it. I never thought I could pull this off again. Angels were all around me, giving of themselves without asking anything in return. C.C., as she always did, had a good idea. With the new job on the horizon, she suggested I resign my position at the pain center and, in lieu of summer childcare for Cleo and Adam, spend the summer with them. I could be a kid with them again, be the dad I always should have been. Sign me the fuck up.

They still had some fun weekly camps that summer, and during that time, I took to splitting three large oak trees that came down on our property into firewood by hand. In the morning, some people do their crosswords, some work out, some meditate. I had my pile of wood. It was physically strenuous, which I liked. I worked out most of my life, which typically requires a certain level of focus, depending on what you are doing. A miscalculation on a weighted back squat, you could damage a knee. A flaw in technique on a max bench press, you drop hundreds of pounds on your neck. The wood was different. Sure, I had to be cognizant of where the pieces might fly after I cut them, but there was just me, my axe, and tons of wood, waiting to be splintered. This was meditation, rumination, and anger management, all rolled into hours of chopping with all my might.

I had a lot of time to think, letting the greatest hits of my life, and biggest flops, roll through my mind. I let them come. Through some I smiled and sighed; through others, I cried, my chopping block a blur. I thought about little moments with my children, like the time Cleo was a baby, no more than three months old, and I was picking her up from daycare. She was in her little high chair and her face lit up when she saw me and made the cutest sound. My heart melted to elicit her joy like that. I wished she would always feel that way when she saw me. Then there was Adam, my fabulous little philosopher with his unblemished honesty. Like his mom, he always speaks his mind. As a boy, he would ask me questions like, "Is Mommy gonna lay more babies?" and "I don't remember swimming in your balls." That one was my fault. I seized these endearing moments and countless others and locked them in my mental memento box, always hoping to add more. I thought how I almost lost that chance when I was gone. I felt gratitude, swinging that axe, that I could be there for them and always would be.

Of course, less golden memories surfaced too. I thought about the opportunities I squandered and the people who swung the axe on me, my reluctant stand-in saviors. They did me favors even though their actions had nothing to do with me. I chipped away at that anger and resentment every day. I still do. That stuff gets rooted in deep and causes us to trip if we cannot rid our path of it. Then, blasting all that wood into warmth, I tried to pare the resentment away from the gratitude that was essential to my life. I was only as good at this task as the number of things I had to be grateful for; and though I had much, that bottomless pit in my soul still yawned. My focus always trained on what I had lost even though, right then, that day, axe in hand, I had all that ever mattered. Another memory shot out like the sparks from my iron hammer contacting a splitting wedge. My life had split into two parts: BA and AA. Life before addiction and after. I found myself longing for the purity of my emotions before every action was not supplanted by the need to increase my dopamine level. I yearned for C.C. and Sloane, BA. Back when we were in college and our love still new, while waiting in line to pay for breakfast at a diner, I pulled C.C. close and kissed her forehead. I did not do it for show, not because I felt like I had to make up for something or overcompensate with affection because of my reluctance to hold her hand in public, as I would come to do in the future. I did it as naturally as a I drew breath. *I wished I held your hand more, love. I wish I took those walks with you. I wish I did more.* A waitress saw and commented on how tender it was, how much it warmed her heart. That was true love for me, that moment. The most natural in love I ever was.

Though I still pined for the old when living in the wonderful new, C.C., Cleo, and Adam were my home, and I was back where I belonged. The fall came and so did my new position as an anesthetist. I was glad to be back at the head of the bed with renewed humility and gratitude. People say money and status are not everything, usually people with none, but I understand the sentiment. In one of her letters to me when I was in the Calvary house, C.C. said she did not care about the loss of my job. She said it did not matter to her, never did, just the love we had. Years later, she was quick to rattle off the resume and financial success of her new love. People also say the first marriage is about love, any that follow are about the money. I understand that now too.

It felt good to get back what I gave away and stand on equal ground with C.C.. I was living as I used to, but now I was sober. Paul, my sponsor, taught me a prayer I still say every night— "Father, thank you for all you have given me, all you have taken away, all you have given back to me, and all you have taken away again." I used to omit the last sentence because I never thought I would need to say it, until I did, but for now, life was good. We took a trip to Hawaii that summer, a Mediterranean cruise the following summer. We worked hard and lived well and the love in our little family, our "Ellis 4," was stronger than ever. Little by little, I stopped—the meetings, conferences with my sponsor, looking in the mirror where all the casualties of my ego swelled like a tumor. There was always that little reservation in the back of my mind that I would drink again. When enough time had passed, when all my wrongs were distant memories, C.C., my kids, my family, would realize I could enjoy life like anyone else.

It was not insanity, it was . . . no, it was insanity. It would not be today or tomorrow or even next week, but with the glacial pace of a horror movie slasher, it would find me again one day, and I would let it come.

Then the probation on my nursing license ended and my random drug and alcohol screens with it. After a few weeks, let's call it six, that little promise I made to myself took the form of a curious bottle of grappa that looked like a glass bong with spider legs. Those quick little lies I tell myself were at the ready; all these five-day workweeks with a two-hour round trip were getting taxing. I deserved the company of an old friend. The grappa, the high-alcohol pomace left over from winemaking, was a hand-me-down from my brother-in-law after he shut his restaurant down years ago and the last shred of alcohol in our house after we went dry. I kept it hidden in plain sight in the basement crawl space. I told myself it was too sentimental to dispose of and that I would give it back to my brother-in-law when I got around to it. One night, after everyone was asleep, I convinced myself he would not miss it. The large cork on the glass spider's abdomen practically crumbled as I removed it. There was not much of the grappa remaining, only seven shots' worth, as it turned out. That familiar fuzz. The catharsis is unparalleled. Every unwanted emotion submerged by those tiny shots. If there is a sense of them, it is a murmuring at best, white noise. The purest peace for a time. There is always the danger of the tomorrow rebound; all the shit is back and now there is guilt and fear and the notion of starting over, but it would be different this time. I am entranced by the trivial again. Banality blurs into something interesting. Relapse does not start with the first drink or drug or whatever it is you cannot just quit. Relapse starts with a plan. I was sober more than three years, at least in body. It was not insanity; it was a choice. It was the same wrong I choice I made over and over.

Let me tell you what happens if we leave our demons shackled in the dungeon, lashing out at us through the bars. If you let them starve rather than come to terms with them and make peace with them, they do not die, they hibernate. My decayed demon, its milky white eyes flicking open after years of waiting, clawed its way to the surface with rotten fingers. Somewhere, I heard a croaking "finally." After those comeback shots, there was the usual twitch of anxiety and shame, but my world kept turning. I knew I could not keep this up. I would eventually get too drunk, and the stench of the alcohol would leak out of my pores. I tried to stuff the demon back in the cage, but it was too big now. I should have talked about it, I should have told my sponsor, I should have told C.C.. But this was my last chance. It was too late for honesty. I wanted my something, but booze was too risky and opiates, my first love, were unattainable, at least in pill form. No, this thought was too crazy even for me.

Let me tell you what happens when you leave those little scraps around for your demons to feed on. Like any good virus, it gets stronger. Chronic, progressive, and fatal. The answer had been in front of me the day I started working as an anesthetist, gaining access to unlimited amounts of IV fentanyl. Honestly, in all my years of practice, I never did consider it. I hated getting needles. Even among addicts, there is a stigma against IV users. I would never be one of *those*, until I was.

Let me tell you what happens if you do not put down your pride and wade out of your shame and ask for help before it is too late. There was absolutely nothing wrong in my life. My kids were healthy, my wife stuck by me through hardships most people would not. Life was good. But I became an IV drug user anyway. Given my skill with inserting needles in other people's veins, I was bad at hitting my own. I vaguely thought it was my dad making me miss. I was about to give up, thinking it was for the best anyway, and then I felt it. That subtle pop of the vein as I broke through the endothelium. A thin tendril of my blood swam into the syringe like a tiny specter. I had the vague sensation I was going to a place I would not come back from. This was the daddy of "I Nevers." I emptied the syringe into my vein. It pushed smooth and cold and . . . *Oh. My. God.*

Nothing Is Trivial

FROM THE PROMISES we make and break, to the advice we give and take, everything we say and do has meaning. Too often, we keep our blinders to the world on, missing those vibrant details that make life interesting. We overlook the gifts from our stand-in saviors and the little lessons we learn from our experiences. Bad ideas manifest into terrible actions. Our petty piles of "I Nevers," "What ifs," and "Fuck its," and our little lies and hatreds and resentments rise till we are buried in them. Our random acts of kindness we receive and pay forward can save lives. Our basal rate of unconditional love is never forgotten. Be it our intention or iniquity, we make an impact on those we care about and those we have never met. We must always do what we say and say what we MEAN (Make Every Act Necessary); no wasted words, no half-truths, and no reckless actions. If we keep our mental memento box full of good things, there is no room for the bad.

11

SPIRITUALLY BANKRUPT

C.C. sat on our wraparound deck in the back of our home, overlooking a half-acre of manicured lawn and another half-acre beyond the fence that ran down to a small creek, where our children would play and discover. It was all ours. It was our dream home. We bought it twelve years ago from a couple going through a divorce. I will never forget the wife arguing with the husband at the closing, pleading with him to cut her a check from the split assets to support their four girls, one of whom was there, sobbing under the weight of it all. That specter of foreboding joy hung heavy on me that day. This would never be us. Until it was. We fell in love with the home instantly with its spacious rooms, detached barn, and sweeping backyard where we would entertain our large extended family. It was a wonderful sight to see friends and relatives and all the people we loved trickling through the gated yard and into our space. That long deck was the perfect place to look out over the dream C.C. and I had made real. This day, it was not a good friend or sister or parent that walked through the gate; it was two men. One was easy enough to spot—he was a policeman. He was escorting another man. He was also a cop but pretended not to be. He was the kind of cop that dresses in cargos and an Eddie Bauer vest and talks to you like he is your buddy until he locks you up for eighteen months. The only escorts I have had were out of career jobs, my most recent about a few weeks before these cops showed up, but we will get to that. The buddy cop introduced himself as a narcotics agent from the Office of the Attorney General. C.C. asked him if I was still alive. Mad love, love.

I was, in fact, alive and back in rehab, again on my heels, backing away from the ripples of the tsunami I had brought down on us. My career as a fentanyl addict thankfully only lasted a few months. I do not think I would have survived much longer than that. I used fentanyl as part of the anesthetics I administered every day. I knew exactly what it did and what the average lethal threshold was. Like most anesthetics, the "blue stuff," as fentanyl was called because of the signature blue label we would use to designate it among other drugs, was relatively short-acting. This predictable perk was important in our practice as a timely emergence from anesthesia was as critical as its induction. This was not a desirable benefit for a drug addict looking for a sustained high. My obsession and compulsion to use were at their most virulent. It was the way everyone should feel except I wanted it all to myself. My tolerance increased quickly, and I had to use more each time, leaving that lethal threshold in my wake. At first, it was only after work, easing the pain of my commute home, then before work, then at home, then at work, which was how I got myself caught again. I call it my "colossal stupidity airbag," activating in the event of my impending death or the death of another at my hands. The high was getting shorter, my respiratory depression, longer. I was weeks or even days away from passing out behind the wheel or going apneic in my sleep. My insanity saved me the day I stuck in a needle in my vein in the locker room at work. When all you care about is that one thing for which you are willing to give up everything, caution is a luxury you do without. A circulating nurse saw me and did the right thing. Another reluctant savior.

That was July 31, 2018, the day to which our divorce was backdated. August 1, 2018, was the day C.C., after bouncing against a glass ceiling for too long, resigned from a twenty-one-year career, one that helped build the remarkable life we had, in search of something befitting her passion and skill. That was also the day I told C.C. what happened. Two increasingly different people, two different choices, one life that was about to end. There is not enough time left to scar over the pain of that day. I knew this was the end. There was no way she would stay with me after this "extraordinary betrayal," as she called it, and rightly so. The ink was not even dry on the Board's vacating of my suspension three months prior. I prove my resolve to be an equal partner again, I get back into my career under insurmountable odds, and I fuck it all up, pulling our life down around our heads again right after she took the second biggest chance in her life; I was the biggest, if that is not obvious. She bet everything on me and believed I had finally found a reason to stay sober and in love. She put her trust in me again, and not to ruin a life of which few even dream. But I chose to do it anyway.

The look on her face this time . . . she said the most horrifying part was that she did not even know. Even with my frequent trips to my safe room in the basement to shoot up, the subtle strangulation of opiates on my voice, she had no idea. I did not want to lose her because I did not know what to do without her but, perhaps for the first time, I took an honest look at what I was doing to her beyond putting pretty apologies on paper. The water torture of countless lies, betrayal, and relapses boring a hole into her soul, drip by drip over years, was abusive. C.C. had always gone through our life, all the happiness and hope she brought contrasting with the antics and agony I contributed. I realized I was going around it, parading around in my masks trying to be what she wanted and deserved. She went through all the pain, and I groveled for her grace again and again, always looking for the easier, softer way. C.C. asked me to let her go, as did one of her sisters. I felt despotic, like my need for her to tell me who I was and my lust for her words of affirmation shackled her to me. I had no identity without her. After all we had been through together, I was still just a man with his masks. She made my life better, and I just made hers harder.

So, another relapse meant another rehab. But as a wise wizard once said, "We're in the endgame now." (Russo & Russo, 2019) We always have another relapse left in us, another backslide into what made our lives unmanageable, but we do not always have another recovery. I knew this would be my last. Still obsessing, not over the delicious mainline euphoria of IV fentanyl but the thrill of the needle hitting home and the plume of my blood in the syringe, after nearly twenty years, I finally accepted this disease would kill me. Avenues Recovery Center would be my final rehab experience, not because I was finally ready to adopt all I have learned into a spiritually fit and fulfilling life, using Avenues' resources to build a solid support network and outreach platform to help others suffering from addiction, finally giving back to a community that has done so much for me. This is my last rehab because I am not going through this shit again. I do not mean the rehab stints themselves. All told, I spent an entire year at Avenues and only left because they could not squeeze any more from my Cobra loot box. If I did not know how to stay sober by now, I never would. I would take what I was given and use it to live whatever life I had left. Or I would die trying.

I would not get another honorable discharge, go back out into the world, stay clean for a while, fuck it up again, beg C.C.'s forgiveness, and go back to another rehab only to rinse and repeat. Even if I was still broken enough to think this endless insanity would go on, instead of breaking the cycle as I promised years ago, C.C. removed herself from it by announcing her plans to divorce me during a couples counseling session. Even though I expected nothing less, it still hurt like shit. Since the final betrayal, I had been more angry than remorseful. Looking back on it with a more lucid lens, I handled it all wrong. I was trying to push her away before she could leave me, a final selfish act to spare my own pain. Throughout our relationship, C.C. would occasionally speak to me in a manner I did not care for. The "C.C. Tone," as I called it, usually came out when I deserved it and I groveled under it like a whipped dog. But it was during more pedantic exchanges, her quips about forgetting the trash or dirty dishes or not servicing the lawn mower, which was now inoperable, and the grass looked like a cornfield, when her sexy, breathy voice went from C.C. to "Karen." It was not what she said, it was how she said it. I loved everything about her except that tone. To this day, she would deny ever speaking to me in that way even though recently, doe-eyed and giddy, C.C. told me her new beau puts a finger over her full lips and gives a playful "shh" whenever she mouths off.

So cute.

Once, though, years ago, she showed me her hand. She was going full-metal bitch on me, when I was in full remission from my addict antics, and in a rare growth of desperation balls, I scrambled up to the tower I placed her on and told her to stop speaking to me like I was one of her underlings at work. She told me she would never speak to someone like that at work. See Chris Rock's "just don't do it" soliloquy in his well-received special *Bring the Pain* to understand my state of mind in that moment. (Rock, 1996) I only bring up my hang-up with this flaw of hers because it was ultimately what caused her to drop the D-word. The two of us were in session with Kelsey, my twenty-five-year-old counselor, whose life experience barely qualified her to rent a car, let alone mitigate the end of a relationship; to her credit, she did not know "divorce Sloane" was on C.C.'s to-do list that day, probably the second or third item down. Kelsey had set up the session with her as a check-in. I do not know if C.C. was looking for one last shred of us in there that day or if her mind was already made up.

Most of our conversations in the months after I was chased down leaving work with a pocket full of fentanyl vials were heated, full of the wrenching emotion you would expect in the gloaming of a twenty-five-year relationship, especially ours, a love so forged by fate, I could not imagine being with anyone else. Maybe everyone feels that way when you find your soul mate, but we were C.C. and Sloane. Until we were not. That day, in our session, she was speaking with a broken heart, but with me swirling in shame and fear, I grabbed the only foothold I could find and brought up the only gripe I had, that she was still talking to me like I was beneath her. I could not let go, so my girl, my love, finally pulled free. She said, "I'm divorcing you." It felt like a physical blow, probably what she had felt for years. I think she said more but all I remember is her leaving and Kelsey saying I needed time alone. I sobbed like a baby. I crawled on the ground and gasped for air. It was exactly what I earned for my actions, but I could not handle the consequences.

I wait for my apocalypse assistant to clock back in, to file it away so I can relive it later when I was ready, but this is too much work. This shit defies filing. I cried for a love and a life wasted. I cried for how selfish and stupid I am. I cried because I could not give her what she wanted and knew she would find another man that would. I cried because, when I left home, I did not know I would never call it that again. I cried because I would only be an every-other-weekend father. I cried for a future that was gone. I cried long and hard to get it all out because I knew the anger would come soon. And I was angry about it and clearly, I still am, my head full of petty and pedantic bullshit. We were above that. We were something special. Now we are a part of the other 50 percent. I am just another divorced "whatever" because I could not be a "who cares." I am still angry about it because I threw away one of the best things that ever happened to me for no fucking reason other than me. But I have no room for it anymore. So, I put it here. Pain has been my greatest teacher, and this was the hardest lesson to learn, but after years of going around it, I had to go through it. Somewhere in the middle of all my tears and snot and emotional muck, I felt relief, learning what I was most addicted to was not a drug at all. My withdrawal from her was worse than any substance.

Just four months ago we took our last trip as the Ellis 4 to a sublime eco lodge in Costa Rica, unfettered by industry and kitschy tourism. It was one of my favorite trips we had as a family. One day, while Cleo and Adam explored the lush stretch of vibrant green unfurling out to the South Pacific, alone in our open-air bungalow, cooled by the tropical mist fan of the rain forest, to the chittering lullabies of Corcovado and the ghost-story groan of howlers, C.C. and I made love. It was the last time we ever would. Three months ago, I would enter rehab for drug and alcohol addiction again for the third time. It was the last time I would ever seek that refuge. Two months ago, I kissed my children goodbye, leaving them and our dream house for the third time in as many years. It was the last time I would call it home. One month ago, with the help of my steady stand-in savior Dina, I was once again granted enrollment in the Board's "lost cause" program to protect a nursing license I did not know if I could ever use again. It would be the last time I was given that chance. Today, curled up on an office floor, would be the last time I would call C.C. my wife.

On to less terminal events, at least those that have not happened yet, and the first of many places I would call home over the next few years, the Avenues recovery crib is a charming farmhouse, sheltered by a giant oak, just outside of my former home in a bullshit suburban utopia full of full-time addicts that are only better than me because they could still afford their luxury cars that sat with mute elegance over a grisly murder, or so it was rumored. One night, me and some of the other boys at "Alms," as we called the house located on "Almshouse Road," set up a Ouija board in the creepy-ass basement to try and get some answers. We were all in different phases of "shoulda-fucking-known-better." There was Devin, the house manager, who used to live in a train station and was now almost two years clean and would do anything for his Avenues clan, including driving hours just to pick up a lost soul trying to find a better way. "American Eric" was only staying clean long enough to get back to a lucrative job at the Port Authority in New York. No judgments here; I still did not know if I was staying clean for something or someone other than myself. He is a good man at his core and funny as shit. Laughing loud and often is a must if you want the most out of life, let alone sobriety.

Say what you will about communicating with the beyond, but at the very least, for guys like us who specialize in deceit, it was a great exercise in trust. Devin flipped through the Necronomicon and the Codex Gigas, otherwise known as the Devil's Bible, on the regular so he was most equipped to preside over finding our murdered ghost. He would begin with a prayer of welcoming and started banging the walls and the furnace to "wake up" any lingering spirits. Everyone had a hand on the heart-shaped planchette, and we started asking questions.

"Is anyone there?" Devin probed. The rest of us chimed in with, "We come in peace," and "You have nothing to fear." The planchette started to move. It was listless at first then definitely started moving toward the "YES" on the board.

"Bullshit," Eric said. "Who's moving it?" I was not. Then we all jumped as Evan, that lovable gorilla who pops your ribs with an affectionate hug, thumped down the creaky stairs. I met Evan a few weeks in as he was being readmitted after a successful discharge. We shared that alpha male weight-lifter sensibility and got along instantly. When I asked why he was back, he replied, "I died," referring to his heroin overdose in a gym locker room. If there was one thing we all had in common, we knew what death looked like. Some, like Evan and Olivia, another Avenues alum who OD'd in the counseling center bathroom, got close enough to smell its breath. Others, like me, have bumped shoulders with it for years, never really paying attention to it, until now. "What are you clowns doing?" Evan half-belched. We told him to shut the fuck up and put a hand on the board.

Channeling the dead takes it out of you, so we recruited other members of the house to sub in. Brandon was a heroin and cocaine addict from a town in "Pennsyltucky," the forgotten stretch of woods and dirt between Philadelphia and Pittsburgh. As his home was located on a landfill, he was fond of saying he grew up as "trash, playing with trash, on trash." Before his discharge, Brandon wrote me a letter thanking me for showing him how to live and that I reminded him of his father, whom he loved and respected more than anyone. I have never received a more endearing compliment. Bo was the young pretty boy with as much ink as he had sober dates, violating curfew to have three-ways at a local hotel. Alex was a decade younger than me, but he was already on a liver transplant list.

The next night, after an hour of accusing each other of moving the planchette, "Rebecca" scrawled her name with our hands and confirmed that it was she who was killed in the house. Our fingers inched along the Hasbro toy slowly, almost melancholic, toward the "YES" with each question. Hey, we all swore we were not moving it. Though our séance was not on the counseling curriculum at Avenues, we were doing the very things that helped us most, listening and sharing. As we focused hard on sliding out Rebecca's truth, we started talking about ourselves, sliding out thoughts we held in even during counseling sessions.

Focus is the best truth serum there is. Lying and deflection take planning and thought. Try it. Do something that requires your full attention. This works best playing a game like Operation (I swear I do not work for Hasbro) where you must devote a large amount of mental energy and physical control to extract plastic organs from small cavities without hitting the sides to the tune of a terrifying buzz. But something like driving stick in a city or playing an intense video game or threading sewing needles or anything you cannot immediately pull your attention from will work as well. When thoroughly engaged with your activity, have a trusted friend who knows most of your dirty secrets ask some hard questions. Let them choose. We spend so much time protecting our lies, taking detours around the truth when the path straight through is always best, we forget what it is to be genuine and speak our truth. When all that energy we use keeping things hidden is repurposed, see how honest and open you get.

Jeff and Gregg became my closest friends there. We stay in touch to this day, and I would not be where I am without them. They got me through my darkest times and split their sides laughing with me in those moments when we were just brothers enjoying being together and alive. None of us were laughing when "Clive" showed up, wrenching the planchette around the board. We assumed he was the big bad Rebecca's murderer, and we had to keep our cool not to threaten to kill the dead bastard again. He never confirmed that he was the killer but the planchette started to pull in different directions. We all said how we felt it being pulled away from our touch. Devin, with the intonation of an exorcist, asked, "Who is this?" The planchette slid with conviction to each letter. First *D*, then *E*, then *V*. "Get the fuck outta here," Eric said, echoing our thoughts, but we all saw the same wide-eyed look in each other. The planchette stayed on its path to *I*, then *L*.

"Nah, man, nope." Eric got up and creaked up the stairs. Devin cautioned we needed to slide the planchette to the "GOODBYE" on the board in unison or the bad spirits could stay trapped in the world. Chris sat in with us this evening and said he would take care of it. Chris was a stoner by trade but used to "boof" (look it up) crystal meth occasionally. After we all got too freaked out to continue our commune with our spectral room-mates, not one for superstition, he nailed the Ouija board and planchette to his wall.

We all laughed and shuddered after our little sit-down with death, but I could not help but think about my own legacy. That night, I had another dream of Dad. He was here, under the oak just outside. His face was old, old as it would have been if he were still alive. With my dream cognition, it made total sense that he was here, Rebecca taking him by the hand to see his son. Fucking Chris, he just dumped God knows who else into the world! He had tears in his eyes. I assumed he was disappointed in me, for how bad I had failed this time. He pointed at my arm. I looked to see my veins swelling out of it. I kept looking with that mute dream-horror, unable to feel or look away. My veins wiggled through my skin, the visceral blue texture taking on a metallic sheen. They went from ropey to stiff and cylindrical. Valves jutted out from veins, now resembling pipes; one of the valves opened. They pulsed and I could hear my heart beating. My other hand moved on its own, bringing a huge steel syringe, its needle dripping feces toward the open valve. I felt so afraid. When I woke with a gasp, I could feel my heart pounding in my chest.

That was not my first drug dream, but it was the most intense. My mind raced to make sense of the nonsensical. My dad was a plumber, thus the pipes in my arm, which were echoes of his soldering lesson and my latent obsession with puncturing my vein, and just hours before we were summoning the dead and he came back to tell me something. *What are you telling me? Do not put shit in my veins?* Okay, obvious. I wanted it to mean something monumental, like Scrooge waking up from his life tour. But here I was still, sharing a room with Tom, a good old alcoholic, older than my dad would have been. Maybe it did not have to mean anything. Maybe I just had to talk about it. So that is what I did.

Poor Rebecca just wanted to talk, to tell her truth. Would I be shoving my way through a bunch of dead people one day to be the first to push a giddy group of friends' hands along a Ouija board, scrawling out my name and my truth? It is said we hang around after our bodies die because we did not accomplish what we wanted or needed to. I think the same applies if your spirit or soul, or whatever it is our bodies shuttle around, dies first. I thought about why I was still here. My body was still going through the motions, but I had no purpose. Did I ever? I wondered if this was how my dad felt in the last years of his life, but I did not have the benefit of dementia. I had reasons I wanted to live, but I was not one of them.

The best thing that can happen to someone like me, so consumed with the mistakes of yesterday and the scarcity of tomorrow, is to take those awful eternities away. I could no longer see my future, my foreboding powers of clairvoyance usurped by ghosts, or clinical depression and the looming fear of a felony conviction, most likely. And the past was getting too painful to play back, my shame of it keeping me from telling my own story and preventing me from listening to others tell theirs. All that was left was today, one day at a time. That aphorism haunted me more than any ghost could, hung in plain sight at meetings, recited in recovery preambles and prayers, even tattooed on a few of my new brothers' and sisters' bodies, some who I got to know long enough to see die. I resisted that dreadful shamble of the day-to-day, going through every moment as it came, pulling my focus from days that did not yet exist and those I could never change. Today never appealed to me, until it did. As much as I craved the chaos of my roller coaster, the simplicity of just worrying about the next twenty-four hours brought me the peace I needed to move forward again.

Some other highlights from Avenues include getting served a divorce settlement on Valentine's Day. I think that is irony, horse therapy, and the rebranding of some of my existing mental disorders and the addition of new ones. For instance, I was a lifelong introvert and proud of it. But we cannot say the "I" word anymore. Now, I am an "INTP-T" under the "MPTI," not an "INTP-A," which seems way cooler, and even though I am supposed to be compatible with an "ENTJ," a yin to my yang, which is what C.C. is but that was bullshit, and now I am with "ESTP," which is not compatible with an "INTP" but we really like each other so the "MPTI" can GTFO. I put as much faith into labels on people as I do about the nutritional label on the bag of horseradish cheddar potato chips I just wolfed down, but it can let you know where you are on the map. The on-site psychiatrist diagnosed with me a "Cluster-B" personality disorder. I could have saved him time and told him I diagnosed myself as a cluster-fuck a long time ago, but a deeper dive proved insightful. Suffice it to say, I checked off most of the boxes on the personality test, the biggest bullet points being "impulsive behavior," "persistent lying," "unstable self-image," "intense displays of anger," and "narcissism." Yup, all that and more.

Though I have mentioned that addiction is a solution to something broken inside us, this was the first time I considered it. I started playing detective with my psyche, poring through the entire battered VHS tape of my life, scanning my timeline of actions and events, trying to determine where it all started. I was reminded of C.C.'s first desperate question almost twenty years ago: "Why did this happen?" I wish I could say those first few pills let the demon off the chain, but I was wearing my masks and lashing out and drowning in shame and insecurity long before then. Like a mass of trauma victims caught in an explosion I helped triage once years ago, limbs and torsos spilled out in our trauma bay, it was impossible to put it all back together. And for me, it did not matter. Setting bones and suturing wounds that were rotten will split apart and look worse than before. I had to scrape off the rusted remnants of old ideas and start over. I am still here, despite my best attempts, and I was beginning to want to be.

I was awarded one more label during my time here, a gift

from my counselor Kelsey, which I turned own personal acronym, SO?, when she confided in C.C. that "Something's Off" with me when poring over my insane actions in the face of the remarkable gifts and support I had in my life. She is not wrong. I defied a definitive diagnosis for years, dumbfounding experts, friends, and family alike. Today, I use it as a mantra. You cannot see the stars till you turn off the lights; I cannot see the good in my life till I turn off the bad. I am not saying you should dictate your life based on extreme expressions of personality traits and emotional defects that everyone on the planet possesses to some degree, but it is important to understand which ones are off the chain. Most mental issues are solved with talk therapy, but some require medication. I shit on the stigma of labels, the contempt before investigation the ignorant give to people in pain, not the diagnoses themselves. My own ignorance to mine kept me sick for a long time. I just could not get over the tragedy of myself. I was fortunate to have extraordinary people help me find my way; we cannot do it alone, but the first person we need to seek help from is the one in the mirror. It must be about you. From there, find people you trust to hear what you have to say. Figure out what is off and then decide if it needs to stay off.

12

GO TO FAILURE

With the lights off, the stars get bright. And at a few thousand feet above sea level, where I and a few dozen other men, wet and shivering in the cold, were lying, some were bright enough to hurt your eyes. Beyond the din of chirping crickets, it was quiet as a cemetery. In a few moments, that would not be far from the truth; we all came here to die. Rick, our narrator of the apocalypse, chronicled our final moments.

"Ready yourselves, men—this is your final battle. Everything you have done in your lives has brought you to this moment."

Distant howls and wild shouts mixed with the chorus of insects.

"You hear them, men? They're coming for you," Rick warned.

The screams grew louder, interspersed with guttural roars and animal growls. Bobby, an Avenues alum like me, lay next to me; I could hear his breath quickening.

"This is it, men! They are at the gates! Fight, men! Fight till your breath is gone and your blood runs red!"

The ground vibrated, the screams were deafening. Silhouettes of men with sticks and spears and swords blotted out the stars. Still screaming and growling, they hacked and stabbed us to pieces. Then they were gone, the grave silence resumed.

"You fought hard, but it was not enough," Rick lamented. "It was the fight of your lives, but you died." The pyre we were lying around was lit, its warmth spreading over us. "Come now and say goodbye to what was."

We all got up (we were not actually killed) and formed a procession line. We all had a piece of paper on which we scrawled the part of ourselves that had caused us so much pain and that we were saying farewell to. "All of me" was scrawled on mine. As we walked past the fire, we tossed it in. It was a powerful symbolic gesture; the last few days here at the SWET (Spiritual Warfare Effectiveness Training) warrior retreat were full of them. Our would-be assailants, staff of the retreat, stood up around us, embracing us and welcoming us into a new life. Not everyone attending struggled with addiction. Some were victims of abuse, military veterans, some slaves to their fear and insecurity, but we were all looking for the same thing: a way to finally break through the wall that was stopping us from walking a path to peace.

It was the fall of 2019. I was successfully discharged from Avenues shortly after celebrating a year sober, working my newest D-Gig as a personal trainer, and living with my mom. As a pleasant aside, on September 2, 2019, I had the pleasure of walking my sister, Helene, down the aisle to wed my newest brother, Rob. I was beyond humbled by her offer to escort her in lieu of our late father. Being the furthest apart of the Ellis siblings, we got along the best. As the youngest in an ACOA family, she has made so much of her life, and I am proud of the beautiful, successful, and happy woman she has become. She made a beautiful bride and I beamed with fatherly love as I lifted her veil and kissed her cheek, salty with tears. Thank you for being you, Helene. I love you.

Back to my spiritual death and rebirth, I heard about the

retreat from Mike, my sponsor at the time. Paul, C.C.'s uncle, was my sponsor throughout my tenure at Avenues. He was the first person I called after the last implosion of my life, and our relationship was the father–son dynamic neither of us was ready for, but both of us needed. Paul was old-school sobriety and made no apologies when holding up the mirror. We spoke every day and bickered like family, but I still journal every day like he suggested and say the prayer he taught me every night. Paul was never a picture of health, and by the time I reached a year sober, it was failing fast. We still stayed in touch, but he was so dedicated to my continued sobriety, he suggested I get another sponsor. Paul died a few years later, surrounded by his family. I said goodbye to him at his funeral; it felt like losing a father. Mike and I met while I was at Avenues, and I was impressed by his brutal honesty and authenticity. We should always seek in a sponsor the things we want and need the most, and I needed both in spades.

The retreat was held in a plot of hundreds of acres in the Poconos, the Pennsylvania "Rockies," all privately owned by a local family. The founders of SWET suffered personal tragedy in their lives and responded by creating a place for others to process and overcome their own. It was a beautiful experience. As much of Pennsylvania is settled over old Native American grounds, the retreat was modeled after their tribal rituals and customs. We learned how these ancestors viewed their lives as a journey through the four seasons, from the spring of their birth to the winter of their death. Our guides explained that we continually cycle through seasons in our own lives, living and dying and being reborn with new perspective, letting go of our past selves. This weekend was all about our rebirth. But we were not finding ourselves; we were forging ourselves. We would start the day as warriors, eating around a fire before migrating to a ceremonial fighting pit. Two men faced off in the ring at a time. We each grabbed a wooden staff and challenged an opponent. I chose Ryan, another young man I knew from Avenues, another man to whom I acted as a reluctant inspiration. I got to know Ryan well on the two-hour ride up to the retreat, sharing my story and listening to his. He was in his early twenties but looked even younger than that, too young to have that haunted look in his eyes, the one you get when you make it out of hell. He looked only a few years older than Adam, and my heart ached for him and Cleo. I spent most of my life resisting my surrogate fathers; now I want to accept my role as one.

We lunge at each other and lock our staffs, pushing against each other with all our strength. Ryan is stronger than his wiry frame suggests; my feet slide back in the dirt. The rest of the tribe watches in silence. Ryan's eyes well with tears, his lips quiver. He lets out a war cry, a raw release of all the shit he has carried to this place. I push him back and shout out my own pain. It starts as a rumble in my belly and revs like an engine up through my throat and out my mouth. Our wild eyes stay locked, and we push, and we scream until tears stream down our faces. We push harder and we scream louder. Cries from the crowd join ours. We scream for a lost youth and a lost love. We scream because we cannot kill the fuckers that abused and molested us. We scream at that reflection in the mirror we can't stand to face. We scream for those who died so that we could be here. We scream because if we could just get out of our own way, we could just live. We scream to get it out; whatever it is, we just get it the fuck out. When are throats are raw and our strength fades, we drop the staffs and embrace, sobbing and thanking each other with hoarse voices. We sit and watch the next challenger and opponent, and the next. It goes on as long as it has to. We were not fighting each other; we were fighting ourselves. We purge our pain into the circle where, in the sun's light, it loses its power over us.

After our cathartic skirmishes, we pile into an authentic sweat lodge for a purification ceremony. Stripped down to undergarments, we sit in the low-profile hut bathed in steam from hot rocks and burning sage. Drums beat, our lodge leader leads us in prayer as we chant, a low rumble with an errant howl from the occasional warrior. The oppressive heat can be dangerous but underpins the goal of getting uncomfortable enough to crack the shell that brings understanding and awakening. Most of us had retreated so far into our own wounds, conscious only of our own thoughts, needs, and pains, we cut ourselves off from the collective strength of others around us. The "sweat" was meant to rid us of the remnants of old ideas and the wreckage of our pasts, making room for our renewed selves. From the lodge, we walked to a nearby stream where we submerged ourselves, baptized in the waters of a new path. It was a seminal experience, renewing the fight in me that had waned over the last few months. But like all my enlightening endeavors—Honduras, Colorado, Avenues—that metanoia was short-lived as I returned to a reality I did not want.

Before choosing nursing as a career path, I considered studying exercise science, so with my nursing career in limbo, again, getting the dime-store equivalent of that defunct dream as a personal training certification seemed like the right path forward. I got a position as a trainer with a high-end gym where I used to work out when I could still afford it. As much as I did not like being around people, I was good at helping them. This was true of me as a nurse and even more so as a trainer.

Ever since I was a fat little kid, with some tough love from my mom and the dawn of puberty, working out gave me purpose. It is a great way to hit bottom every day if you do it right. From lifting weights in my basement on my own, with a picture of Arnold in mid-bicep curl for inspiration, to winning and losing with teammates, the combination of adrenaline and attention was more intoxicating than any artificial high. The only time I stopped working out for any significant stretch was when I was actively using opiates. The first step in getting your mind right is to get your body right. Resistance training is best, I think. It requires focus, finding that mind-muscle connection, and you get the most bang for your buck. Cross-fit is fine, too, but can be too intense if you have never exercised before. Just do not become a runner; runners are worse than addicts.

If you have ever paged through a fitness rag, you have no doubt seen programs with promises of "the last [insert body part] workout you will ever need," flush with pictures of fitness models that have never done said workouts. There are neatly detailed instructions, including sets, reps, rest intervals, undulating periodizations, diet tips, and blah, blah, blah. Occasionally, though, instead of rote secret strategies like "3 sets, 10 reps" (yawn) or "rest 60 seconds" (wake me when it's done), there is just "TF," or "To Failure." Now we are talking. Do not get me wrong. There is a method to every madness and every workout routine, but I have only had one rep scheme: go until I can't go anymore. To this day, with rare exception, I am up at 4:00 a.m. almost every day to ensure I have enough time to kill myself so I can live. With metal in my ears, I toss iron around, pushing, pulling, squatting, sprinting until I am drenched in sweat and my breath rattles in my lungs. Sitting on a bench, spent, my body so engorged with blood my skin feels like it will tear, I have never been more at peace.

Without realizing it, I was perverting this failure principle in other aspects of my life, continuing to use drugs and abuse my loves to see how far I could go, how close to the bottom I could get. After my recent attempt at failure with fentanyl, my mother asked me if I wanted to die. Almost none of us commit suicide. Almost all of us self-destruct. In some way, in some part of our lives—we drink, we smoke, we use drugs. We do things we know we should not. We destabilize the good job, the happy marriage —these aren't decisions; they're impulses. Destruction is in our DNA. It is as if apoptosis, or the necessary programmed death coded into every one of our cells, subverted my higher functions, rendering me into a walking bomb. Despite my actions to the contrary, I want to live; so, I try every day to kill the parts of me that want me dead, in the gym and in meetings, so the rest of me can carry on.

I modified my failure principle for my clients at the fitness club. The sun gleaming through skylights, walls of windows, and aisles of treadmills and ellipticals were not my scene. I was raised in dingy gyms with rusty plates and steel bars welded into improvised benches and squat racks. But I still knew how to get people in shape. Being a lifelong athlete, I took for granted how many people in gyms, or anywhere, do not know how to use their bodies. They do not know which muscles perform which functions and often sabotage their own fitness goals. No judgments here—it just helped adapt my approach to getting clients on the right path, and I enjoyed it. It felt good to be part of something I knew again, lending my knowledge and perspective to help someone improve themselves. Throughout my life, I was generous with my time to friends and strangers alike when they asked for tips to improve their workouts. Better late than never, I realized when you are good at something, never do it for free; but with the bullshit give-and-take pay structure of the club, it felt like I was. My position as a "FitPro" became less about training and more about sales, which I could not stand.

There was a fun career to be had, but even with all my masks, I lacked one with tacked-on chicklet teeth and endless exuberance. I was there to train, not to sell. Once again, I became disenchanted with a would-be dream job that was not what it seemed. I tried; I really did. I tried to be grateful and humble, and I went above and beyond, designing programs on my off hours and going in to train clients on my off days, waiting for this whole thing to click. I just could not get over the fact that I was barely making minimum wage; my ego began to groan. I could barely live on my own with a six-figure job, and I was beginning to glimpse a future where whole families are content with much less; but not me. Yes, money cannot buy you everything, but it can buy you an attorney who can turn a felony conviction into a misdemeanor and that I would not have saved up had I been a personal trainer. Yeah, I avoided a cell and the death sentence of a nursing career but not that of my relationship with C.C., to which I vainly hoped we could rekindle. "You get away with everything," she said to me when I told her the verdict. It sounded like good-bye. We stopped talking about us after that, no more veiled anger and groveling on my part, no more mute reservation on hers. The emotional tectonics of the last year had set a permanent rift between us. It was all about Cleo and Adam now. C.C. was moving on, as she had to. Her last text to me:

BECAUSE OF HOW *I'm built (people do what they say they're going to do), it's hard for me to accept—I didn't get what I wanted—you, but honest and intimate. I'll get over it eventually. This is what I deserve in my life and it doesn't seem to be you. Hard realization for me. Sorry . . . but that's my truth. I believe now (my rock bottom) that you're not capable or that you didn't care enough to be that man for me. It is what it is. But you just threw away a very precious gift.*

C.C. DID THE HARD WORK. She went through it while I was still going around it and getting away with it. I did not know who I was anymore. My government cheese insurance decided it would not cover my antidepressants any longer. A month later and the emotional erosion from the Effexor was wearing off. Grief was finally setting in. I would not let it. I beat rehab, beat a felony, and I beat marriage. Fuck redemption, fuck life, and fuck love. I was alone and probably always would be, probably always should be. I caged my heart in anger and it stayed locked in there. Only my kids had the key.

I was grateful to my mom for letting me stay with her while I figured things out, but after six weeks of looking at the Star Wars wallpaper in my old room, the "forty-five-year-old-virgin" look was getting old. As a wise convict once said, "Get busy livin' or get busy dyin." (Darabont, 1994) My cousin, Billy, was like another brother to me. We bonded over the summer of 2000 down the Jersey shore when we and some of my other "heavy hitters"—brothers, cousins, and friends—would drop ecstasy and go to foam parties. Now that was a spiritual experience. A few years younger than me, since high school, Billy was always a drinker. But you are not an alcoholic until you get caught. Billy never got caught, not the way I have been many times, but a lost love here, a nomadic existence there, and life eventually boxed him in. He had his first withdrawal seizure during the summer. He went to rehab and had about four months sober. He had just gotten out of a complicated long-term relationship and suggested I move in with him and his lovable boxer, Bodhi. Two broken men and a dog healing through commiseration. What could go wrong?

The day I moved in, Billy was there with his parents—my godparents—my aunt and uncle. My uncle was the closest I had to a father after my dad died. He never gave up on me and was the biggest champion of my sobriety even though his own definition of dry was drinking Coors Light. They stopped by the house often and I was glad to spend more time with them. Before I could get curious about why Billy was just chilling with his parents in daylight on a weekday, he told me he lost his job on account of being drunk during business hours. Having lost three of my own that way, I could not give him a hard time, but two problems were apparent. My rent was only half of his mortgage payment and, barely a year sober myself, I was moving in with an untreated alcoholic. Still, I thought the arrangement was best for us both; if I was going down again, better to do it with family.

After a day of training clients, I would return home to see Billy on his laptop and phone, working contacts and looking for jobs. We would hit recovery meetings together during the week, take turns making dinner, and laugh long and loud at stand-up comedy specials on Netflix. We were the perfect little odd couple.

After a few weeks, I came home to find Billy asleep on the couch, but not in the casual repose of an afternoon nap; with his mouth gaping and his body contorted in a position only excessive alcohol would leave you, he was passed out. I felt the way I did when I would see my dad like that. Bodhi was curled up on the couch next to him, almost scared. I scratched his square jaw, gave him a treat, and went to a meeting. I asked Billy about it the next day and he said he was just exhausted. I was not ready for this. I felt sick when I saw him lying there like that but envied him at the same time. I did not like my days, nor did I enjoy my nights. My only joy was seeing Cleo and Adam. She was growing into a beautiful woman, he into the man of the house, their house. It was still the "Ellis 4," but I had been replaced by a dog. It was hard going back there, especially now that it was changing as renovations were underway, but it was the only way to see them. Our custody agreement was one-sided, and with my history, I did not have much ammunition to fight it—not that I could. I had no place to take them; I would not bring them to Billy's.

Sometimes I would take them into town to the comic shop or for some ice cream, but I was content just to be with them, no matter what we did. But being there was a constant reminder of what I had given up. I started to think about what it would look like when they got older and co-parenting and graduations and weddings and a new stepfather . . . fuck, how would I handle that? C.C. was moving on, and I could not. I felt left behind. The grief started twitching again so I crammed more anger and resentment down its throat. There was a faint din of gratitude over being where I was. I could still see my children; I was employable, another AA buzzword until it was my reality; and C.C. was "okay" in the sense that my betrayals and abuse of her life and trust did not break her—not that I ever could; she was too strong. But that virtue was all but drowned out by my roaring resentment of myself, which I projected outward. I was still in counseling, back with Babette, and I was talking about my fears and the thin thread my sobriety was hanging from. Desperation honesty is still honesty. I always left the sessions with hope, and I tried hard to hold onto it, but it was swallowed up by that hole I would never fill. I knew I was going to a house that did not feel like a home and to a job I did not like, and I had no one to blame but myself.

Fucking Apple—throwing up anniversary photos from a few years ago and other times when life was good and we were together. One morning I got up and there was a selfie of the two of us in Hawaii, happy, her face lit up with that amazing smile. I tossed the phone at the wall. I had to pull from my savings to get another. Please remain angry and depressed. Everything was not going to be okay.

That day at the club, I was in between sessions and walking the floor. "Be seen to get the green," was a motto club members would not see on the website. I expected no green while being seen, nor did I expect to see a man lying on the floor in the lounge area next to a comfy sofa. I have seen people do some strange shit in gyms but clawing at their chest and gasping for air like a fish out of water was a first. My body started to move on its own. Fear, anger, sadness, doubt, all of it gone the instant I saw that guy on the ground.

I fell to my knees by his head and made a clamp with my index and middle fingers behind the angles of his jaw and my thumbs along his mandible and pulled up, performing a jaw thrust. This serves two functions: 1. It lifts the tongue and soft tissue off the trachea, opening the airway, and assesses level of consciousness. 2. It HURTS. Unless the affected individual is dead or close to it, they will get pissed and try to pull my hands away. The obstruction to his airway broken, he gasped out a shuddering breath but nothing else. I yelled to a trainer at the desk to call a code "100," our super-secret club code for a member in distress. I slid my fingers to the carotid pulse in his neck. Nothing. My right hand clasped itself over my left and they both moved to his sternum on the mid-areolar line. My arms stiffened into pistons and started compressions, depressing his chest 1.5 to 2 inches at 100 bpm, hard and fast. Others started to arrive. The resident CPR expert, a nineteen-year-old lifeguard, stood beside me with oxygen, a face mask, and eyes wide as saucers. I grabbed the gear and told her to get on his chest. She was jackhammering his chest, going too fast; the blood trapped in his heart was not going where it needed to. Calmly, I told her to sing "Staying Alive" in her head, giving a deep compression with every "ah, ah, ah, ah," and to keep that cadence. She sang it out loud, but she was doing it right with a rate around one hundred beats per minute; my pulse was barely above sixty.

I began breathing for the patient with the oxygen bag and mask. I gave the patient a breath every time I took one, which was about every four seconds to prevent air from trapping. I looked at another trainer and told him to call 911 if they had not already, and I asked another to grab the AED. Onlookers were clumping in a circle, and I asked the security dude on duty to start crowd control. The AED arrived, and my hands, still on autopilot, placed the defibrillating pads, one under the right clavicle, medial to the nipple, the other on the lower left chest, beneath the pectoral muscle in the mid-axillary line without even looking at the visual aids. I fired up the machine and we listened to its prompts. I told Emmy the lifeguard to keep singing and pressing until the machine said to hold. The robot voice on the AED advised a shock and gave a "clear the patient" warning. Emmy looked at me and I gave her a nod to back away. My finger over the glowing red button, I said for the first time in years, "Clear!" I hit the button and the man's body convulsed once, his hands thrown up almost in frustration. He coughed and sputtered and puked. I called for everyone to roll him on his side. I kept the oxygen on his face. He was moaning and spitting, but he was breathing. He was alive. EMS showed up and took it from there.

After I gave a statement to the accompanying police officer, I joined the code team; everyone was buzzing with adrenaline. The general manager of the club was there, and he held out his hand. "You're a hero," he said. That practiced compartmentalization in place, I shook my head and I almost said, "It's my job." But it was not anymore. I said "thank you" but I still marginalized my involvement, saying everyone else did the heavy lifting. He smiled and cut me off. "Sloane, you're a hero." Emmy took my other hand almost with reverence, thanking me for my help. The others gathered around slapping my shoulders, smiling and shaking their heads, and giving me those encouraging words I say I do not need but really do. "Hero." That metaphysical role that I was supposed to play but always rejected. Here I am with full sunshine beaming through the vaulted skylights of a bougie boutique gym surrounded by eyewitnesses calling me a hero and still downplaying it. "It's what I was trained to do," "I've done that a thousand times," "I am not a special butterfly." But for a few heartbeats that day, I let it in; it felt like those few moments of weightlessness as the roller coaster begins its descent. I am a fucking hero. I would enjoy it while it lasted because I knew it would not.

13

. . . OR DIE TRYING

Three days later, it was Thanksgiving, and I was sitting in my cousin's bedroom, the place he graciously let me make my home, with his gun pressed to my head. It was a steel beauty, a 9mm Glock 34, which, at this range, could fire a bullet in one side of my head and out the other. I pulled back on the slide and let it snap back into place. I imagined the boldface onomatopoeia of a comic book sound effect—*CH-CHAK*. I pulled the trigger. *Click*. A clip loaded with jacketed hollow points sat on the bed next to me. Billy only had range rounds meant for ease of use with low recoil while practice firing. Because these bullets do not expand or fragment on impact, I have seen people survive one to the head; I could not take that chance. I went out and got a box of the real things. When we glimpse the end of something, we tend to think about its beginning. I have glimpsed so many ends and contemplated so many beginnings, I no longer care where it all started, only when it will all end. I was going to end it that night. Billy and I ate dinner with our extended family at our aunt and uncle's home. Billy wrote a very touching poem to his parents; the paper he wrote it on trembled as he read from it. Cleo and

Adam were with C.C. and her family. Along with a lopsided division of assets, we would also divide holidays; another reminder of how life would be moving forward. Despite all I should be thankful for, I still focused on all I had lost. No, I did not lose anything; I gave it all away. That realization did not make it any more palatable. *CH-CHAK. Click.* The pulpy graphic novel sound of the cold steel reminded me of another beginning, one I also hoped would be the last. Just a few months ago, still at Avenues, my discharge was imminent, and I got a going-away present in the form of a sobriety shock tactic.

I'm sitting in a circle of people I have come to care for very much on one of those office chairs with wheels and a lever that brings you up and down. Katy struggles to get her eyes, shrink-wrapped in tears, to meet mine. She squirms in her seat, crimping her mouth tight, looking anywhere but at me. She lets out a frustrated sigh. She isn't frustrated with me, I don't think, but with what she was just asked to say to me. Finally, her ocean-blue irises wash over me, soft with pity. "You are a lying, self-centered bastard," she says, shaking her head. A tear breaks loose. Her face melts with apology. I turn my chair a hair to the left to face Sebastian, another housemate. The hydraulics click through the chair's shaft. *CH-CHAK. Click.* Never one to shy away from the bare-knuckle truth, evenly, he says, "You never loved us." Another turn of the office chair, another *CH-CHAK*, another *click*. I stop at Gregg. He rubs the stubble on his cheek then drops his hand in his lap. His Sunbeam Bread Boy face betrays a violent criminal past. I love him like a brother. He flashes a conciliatory smile full of chicklet teeth and says, "You abandoned us." Another turn, another *CH-CHAK*, *click*, just like the gun I keep cocking and putting against my head. Now Angela, a deer in headlights, says, "You're a bad father." I hear the words but it's like they are aimed at someone else. *CH-CHAK. Click.* Jen says, "You've ruined every good thing you've ever had." *CH-CHAK, click.* "You can't be in a loving relationship." *Click.* Dylan, his face down, peers up at me. "You always come first." I keep turning. *CH-CHAK, click*. "You're reckless." *Click*. "You drove drunk with your kids." *Click*. "Something's off." *Click*. "You just couldn't get it done." *Click*. "You'll never be present." *Click*. "You chose this." *Click*. "You'll always be alone." *Click*. "I hope it was worth it." *Click*. "You don't want to be sober." *CH-CHAK, Click. Boom.*

"Torture, isn't it?"

Hush puppies press into the microfiber carpet as a man saunters outside the circle of shame. John Shepard, the celebrant in this Church of Chastising, head counselor of Avenues Recovery Center, delivers the message of his existential experiment.

"To hear that committee in your head all the time," he continues, one of his lanky arms draped by his side, the other bent upward, his thumb pressed against his first two fingers. "To let it tell you who you are. Pure torture. It's not real, but we spent all our lives listening to it so it's the only truth we know."

Intense and affable, John scans the circle then looks straight at me. He brings out the best in those who have indulged the worst in themselves; not always gently. "Now everyone look at him and keep repeating what you just said." My brothers and sisters in recovery, my reluctant jury, look at each other, and me, with dread.

"C'mon, speak up," John urges. The accusations resume. My sins, scattered in the intonations of my friends, blend into a listless undertone.

"Louder," John tongue-lashes the circle. The voices are staggered like the beginning of a hymn no one knows, but I can hear my truth again. I turn and click around the circle to look at my friends; no one is looking back.

"Louder!" Faces turn to John in frustration. Voices crack the way they do when throats are yanked by the collar. I look at Katy, tears streaming down her face; I choke back my own. Gregg is looking right at me, bless his melting heart and face. Even Sebastian seems sorry. This cacophony of scorn continues because it must. I need to hear it. I need to feel it. We all do. My tears are for them as much as myself. Will this feeling, this catalogue of all my sins spoken, change me? Can I channel this pain when I am weak? I was never weak; I just didn't want to—

"Stop!" yells John.

The chorus is replaced by sniffling and shuddered breaths. "That's what a syringe full of heroin does." John scans every eye, dry and wet. "That's what a fifth of vodka does. That's what a line of coke does. It makes it stop. All the pain, the doubt, the fear, all the shit we let ourselves believe. Gone. And nothing, not a family, a job, or fear of a cell, can compete with that."

John looks at me. "So, keep using, keep the committee quiet." John looks around the room again. "But every time you do, you're putting a gun to your head and daring yourself to pull the trigger. *Click*. Best case, you wind up back here, if you're lucky."

I pressed the muzzle against my head.

It is fascinating what your mind does to segment all the unwanted emotions, what it latches onto to stem the mounting tide of anxiety and depression. Imagining my face shattering against the windshield or a crimson chunk blowing out the back of my skull became soothing. I was caring less about what my family would think. People die every day; I would just fade into another statistic. C.C. would hate me, if she already did not, but she would get over it. Then I would think of my children and what it could do to them. I watched my dad kill himself. It was a slow suicide, but it felt the same as finding a loved one with their wrists open in a bath full of blood when it was all over and look what that did to me. They did not deserve that, but I could only feel my own pain right now. Our dominant thoughts become our actions.

"But life is impossible for you, right? You're not broken— everything else is." John walks his slow circle. "So, you keep drinking, you keep snorting oxy, you keep pumping your veins full of heroin because you just can't bear to live." The room is a tomb. "And then you die, choking on your own vomit, or with a noose around your neck, or with your head splattered against the wall. You're dead but it's just beginning."

I have more suicide notes than attempts. I never planned, but I would frame it out in a mental movie, complete with a dramatic soundtrack full of tinkling piano keys and low detache notes on the cello. C.C. called my bluff once. It was the first few months after the extraordinary betrayal and I was being dramatic and said something like, "I only know one way out," with pretend conviction. C.C. said, "Then go ahead and do it." Bitch knew I was bullshit, but at that point, I could not blame her for saying it or wanting me to go through with it. I did not have access to a gun, until now, but I would google the best position to put a firearm to ensure I would not miss and rot on a ventilator as I no longer had a power of attorney to pull the plug, only to be met with a suicide hotline number. I suppose they offer the most ad money. I had fired a gun before, much like the one I was holding now. My brother is an expert marksman and taught me how to use it. I remembered the raw power in such a small thing. Whatever was in front of it, went it went off, was destroyed. I could relate.

The first time I experienced the shock of suicide was in high school. A classmate was found dead in his bedroom, an empty bottle of painkillers, opiates I assume, sitting on top of a note. That was the story that was whispered through the halls. The official announcement at our morning assembly was that he "died suddenly," a metaphor for suicide I would see in obituaries from time to time. It happens much more than you would like to imagine. I knew the kid. He was quiet, kept to himself during lunch, and was never in trouble. I could not understand how bad your life could possibly be to do that to yourself, until I did.

John Kane resumes playing the tape on what happens after you take the easy way out. "Days go by, and no one has heard from you. Your phone rings next to your rotting body. A friend or a parent goes to your house and bangs on the door," John's eyes get wide, perhaps in remembrance. "They're desperate so they kick the door in. It stinks; you've been dead for days and now your mom or your dad or your kid sees your body."

I let the image fill me up till it leaks out my eyes and I weep for a beautiful life I pissed away for no reason. I had every chance to make it right and then some and I kept taking them for granted. I did not deserve them, and they did not deserve me. On a day of gratitude, all I had was resentment. What a waste; what a fucking waste.

"Your son or your daughter, they scream 'why?' and they'll never be right again because your final lesson to them was to give up. Your mom or your dad must bury their child now, wondering what they could have done different. Your husband"—John looks back at me—"or your wife, what will they say?"

She would not say anything she had not already said to me. She did everything she could. She would take Cleo and Adam and move on; she would get through it, as she always has. The only way out is through and if the love and grace and hope and gifts I received throughout my life and the lessons I learned over and over could not get through my skull, then a fucking bullet would. *I am so sorry, my loves, I just cannot feel this way anymore.* This was the only solution I ever needed. I loaded the clip and slammed it home. *CH-CHAK*—then a sneaker bounced around in the dryer.

At least that was what it sounded like. But the dryer was two floors down. I heard it over the loud rasping noise I realized was me breathing. I pulled the gun away from my head and slid the clip out. I pulled the slide back —*CH-CHAK*—expelling the loaded shell. I opened my door and looked down the hall at Billy's door; something was rattling it on its hinges from inside. I crept to the door and gave a knock, calling Billy's name. The hinges still rattled. I pushed it open, but there was something blocking it. I stuck my head in to see Billy, his body curved into a yoga "boat" pose. He was making those muted gasps you make when you are under water and running out of air. His lips were turning blue. He was either crushing his core or having a grand mal seizure. I decided it was the latter. In the most awful moment of déjà vu I have ever had, I dropped to my knees and nearly yanked his jaw off his face. His airway gasped open, and froth bubbled from his mouth. He was still convulsing, but he was moving air. I held his jaw open for what felt like the rest of the night. When the seizure finally passed, I laid him on his side to let the mucus drain. For a moment I was a teen again in my basement, watching my dad getting through a seizure, his body heaving as it shed its rage like the Hulk changing back to Bruce Banner. Trauma is trauma. Billy came out of his postictal state and stared at me. I brought him back to baseline, telling him where he was and what happened. He was scared but finally said he was "fine."* Poor Bodhi, he came over and started to lick Billy, fixing him the only way he knew how. We just sat there for a while, two broken men and a dog.

We are taught to seek a higher power, not so much to rid us of our pain and misfortune but so we can accept there is something greater than us. I believe in a higher power. I have seen it work though my angels and my saviors in the world, but even after years of Catholic school and Bible readings and the power of prayer, I never could believe in a supreme being that could reach down and guide you when you had gone so far off your path. I believe my dad was there that night to give his son one more chance. Everything I did, all the pain I caused, all the betrayals, the lies, the recklessness, allowed me to be there to save that man's life in the gym, and now probably Billy's life. Maybe someone else would have found the gym guy, maybe Billy would have made it through, maybe it is just a way to rationalize all the horrible choices I made. It is said nurses are called to their profession; for me it was the biggest D-Gig of all, but that night, I finally agreed with that sentiment.

The next day, I talked to Dina at the Board and asked her

what I needed to do to work as a nurse again. I had been out of work for more than a year and the odds of getting back in with my very extensive history of fuckups was not good. The adage "nurses eat their own" does not apply to nurses in recovery. Alicia, another angel, and one of the nurses in my Livengrin outpatient group, worked at a subacute vent facility, which was a nursing home where most of the residents were comatose and/or on permanent ventilatory support. It was the kind of nursing position I dreaded taking as a new graduate, but now, with my newfound humility and lease on life, it was mother's milk, or tube feed, the predominant method of nutrition at the home. I made my case to the Board, Alicia talked me up to the Director of Nursing at the nursing home, and I put scrubs on for the first time in two years.

The vent facility was a spurting, retching kick in the perspective. As most were dependent on ventilators for survival, may residents had a tracheostomy, an artificial airway cut into their throat, below the vocal cords. Consequently, most could no longer swallow food, so a feeding tube was inserted directly through the abdomen into the stomach or intestine. These portals to sustenance would fail from time to time and the results were gross, to put it mildly. It was a position I did not want, but sorely needed and was grateful to have. Most of the residents— this was their home—were middle-aged or older, suffering from debilitating neurological and muscle-wasting diseases. Many were permanently comatose, their families or the state keeping them alive because no one could make the decision to let them die. Some were conscious and lucid and just wanted life support in their final years. There were a few, however, who were younger, one under the age of eighteen. He went into cardiac arrest from a drug overdose and was revived too late for his body to resume breathing on autopilot. He did not want to be there on that machine. With his one functioning arm, he kept trying to pull his tracheotomy out and let nature do the rest. That could have been me.

On paper, it was a somber place, but dedicated families, some who saw their debilitated loved ones every day, the staff, and even some of the residents themselves brought much hope to what was otherwise a physically and mentally exhausting twelve-hour shift. In the majority of positions I held as a nurse, at most I would care for a patient no more than a week; as an anesthetist, I would provide care no more than a few hours. At the Home, I felt like a live-in caregiver for these men and women, caring for many for the entire duration of my employment there. Many of the residents had been there more than a decade. In many ways, what I did there was the essence of what nursing is, and what I dreaded the most. My time at the Home reminded me that this was in my nature, that despite all my faults, I was an empathetic person at heart. I did not agree with the non-life many of these people had, but it was not my choice; I was there to do what I apparently did best. It is a profession I did not want, but it kept wanting me. I left there many days wanting to quit, but I realized this was probably the best I could hope for, given my choices. I kept telling myself I was fortunate to be there and to remain grateful. That mindset was not always easy to keep. Still, I had a steady paycheck and met some wonderful people there, like Theresa, a beautiful human being and nurse's aide who crooned through the shift, singing everything from Marley to gospel songs. It was people like her that gave the Home a soul, making it more than a morgue with a pulse.

Then came Covid. It started with news of emerging cases reported with deaths involved. It did not take long for the media, using every social weapon at their disposal, to turn the slow trickle of paranoia into a deluge of hysteria. The death toll, while tragic, was not the biggest fallout of the pandemic; it was the erosion of society. Taking away restaurants and bars and Starbucks, disrupting the patterns we did not realize we rely on as much as the air we breathe, now through masks, we realized how fragile our sanity is. Then take away jobs and throw in a public execution of a black man, causing decades of racial tension to snap, and the country tore itself apart.

As a recovering drug addict, I took strange comfort in the pandemic. People like me have been living in a personal apocalypse for years and we adjusted to the mayhem better than most. Like many who adapted and relegated their communication with the outside world to FaceTime and Zoom, my counseling sessions and meetings followed suit and we did not miss a beat. With the death toll from the virus continuing to rise and quarantine no longer a word thrown around only in dystopian films, not to mention my position on what was becoming the front line of infection, C.C. and I decided that I not visit Cleo and Adam until we knew how bad things would get. An outbreak of the "Kung-Flu" in a nursing home would spread like wildfire and cause just as much damage. Among the fearmongering stories in the news was one about mass deaths in nursing homes in surrounding counties and states, one with an image of body bags with no vacancy piled up in their alley. The fear was palpable.

Besides our work shifts at the Home and trips to the grocery store, the staff at the Home were mandated to stay in their houses—not that there was anywhere to go. By then, Billy was back in rehab and Bodhi went to stay with my aunt and uncle. For the first time ever, I was alone. For months, I woke up, did what I could to kill myself through an obscene number of push-ups and pull-ups on a door sill, went to work, went back home, watched a movie or played video games, and went to bed, only to wake up and do it all again. At a glance, for someone who craves solitude like me, the pandemic seemed a dream come true. But after a few weeks of being alone in Bo's house, in which my most endearing memories were of both of us nearly dying a few months prior, the darkness began to set back in. I still talked to my kids every day and prayed every night that they stayed healthy. I started to spiral; I missed the emotional erosion of antidepressants. I started to hate the world again, which, for me, went from a place ravaged by a plague we did not understand to one that had it coming. I did not care about what was in the news, only that it was bad. Traffic was nonexistent and liquor store lines were long; I was getting scared, but not of a virus. So, I started picking up extra shifts at the Home. Between the prohibition of anyone except staff and residents in the facility and the standard six feet of social distancing imposed on everyone, the Home became more somber. Every day, we feared an outbreak, but to the staff's credit, for more than a year we kept it free from a single case of Covid-19, long enough to get every resident and staff member vaccinated—those who consented to the vaccine, that is, but that is a story for another book.

There was an "honor among the broken" air about much of the staff; many of us there had a past, and though a few of us confided in each other, no one asked, and no one told. It was not easy to keep places like the Home staffed as turnover is constant. There were a few fine old-school nurses that had been there for decades and loved their jobs, but most were just passing through, looking for something else. Recovering addicts like me, disgraced nurses who came from a more acute care background, brought an uncommon level of skill to skilled nursing facilities like the Home; as such, warts and all, we were brought on as bargain-bin remedial rock stars. I am not a special butterfly. I had to relearn many of the essential skills to do my job there, but former ICU nurses like myself and John, a man who shared the same fall from grace as I, responded to a few critical situations in the Home where the resident may have died without our intervention. John and I developed a strong bond in our time there. We were from different backgrounds—he was former military and lived a nomadic lifestyle, much like my brother—but we shared many of the same interests and he became my closest confidant. Every shift together was equal parts employment and twelve-step meeting.

Being able to commiserate and counsel each other each week did more to ingrain sobriety in me as a way of life than years of formal treatment. As much as I craved solitude, millions of years of instinct cried out for bonds with others. In his book, *Chasing the Scream: The First and Last Days of the War on Drugs*, Johann Hari contends that the opposite of addiction is not just sobriety, but "connection." (Hari, 2015) We are a pack species—we cannot live in any meaningful way alone, despite how long I tried. I formed many bonds through my life and rehab experiences but never held onto them; I never embraced their necessity, until I did. "When the pupil is ready," I suppose. The bond I've shared with John and others since is a big reason why I am where I am today. We remain close friends and brothers. Most of the staff there looked to John and me for guidance just because of our grace under pressure and how we acted on the inherent instincts we developed in our former careers. It felt good to be part of a team like that and accepting a position as a leader that I had inherently rejected for decades.

John also brought me into a nursing support group in which he was a member. There I met Karen, also an anesthetist in recovery with long-term sobriety. She told me her employer had a tolerance for people like us and asked me to consider talking to her chief anesthetist. I did not think that returning to the profession was a possibility, let alone in my best interests. To even be considered to work as an anesthetist again, I had to work as a registered nurse for one year without incident; I still had six months before I could even petition the Board. Then there was the additional baggage I'd accumulated since my last job, a mountain of explanations I would have to provide for a "yes" answer that would not fit on the three additional lines provided under questions people usually answer "no" to on an application. I thanked Karen for the little taste of improbable hope, but I could not bring myself to feel it. I was focused more on the hope of what was in front of me. With the pandemic hitting a relative plateau and the vaccine incoming, after weeks of Adam asking me when I was coming over and me fighting back tears, I was able to finally see Cleo and Adam again. The reunion was a high peak on the roller coaster. All the horror and the fear and the depression of the last few months were gone the moment I saw them. They just make me better.

By then, having a more reliable cash flow, I realized that in my rush to get married, buy a dream home, and vacation home, I had never crossed "renting my own apartment" off my bucket list. Billy had just returned home from rehab and the writing was on the wall that, even with what I was paying him, he could not hold onto his house; we both agreed it was time to move on. I thanked him for his generosity and apologized for not doing more for him. As much as I know that we must make the choice to live or die on our own, I still felt responsible for his relapse. Of course, he told me that was the furthest thing from the truth, and he understood that I needed to move on. Win or lose, I needed to take full accountability for my life, even though I was practically middle-aged before I did. And I wanted a space to share with Cleo and Adam if they wanted it. I found a modest two-bedroom apartment in Norristown, PA, miles from the first home C.C. and I owned and where Cleo was conceived. It looked like a gulag from the outside, but the inside was nice enough. It was close to work, the rent was affordable, and it felt good to have my own space. By then, my kids were entrenched with their friends and their schedules and did not want to do the every-other-weekend thing. It hurt because it finally hit home how much of their lives and growth into teens I had missed, but I understood. I compromised by bringing them over every other Sunday or so for the day. It did not matter what we did or for how long, just as long as we were together.

Then came Anna. We first met as classmates in anesthesia

school almost fifteen years ago. There was an immediate attraction between us, but at the time, I was happily married, and she was happily engaged. Still, we formed a close bond during our training. After graduation in the fall of 2006, she went onto a happy life of marriage and four children, and I, well, just page through the last few chapters. I did not see Anna again until I went to a healthcare support group at Livengrin in 2018. I was already addicted to fentanyl, but I was still trying to keep up appearances. In the pre-meeting, outside of the room, where people got their last smokes in before an hour of hope, Anna came up to me with a smile.

She had been through a tough few years. She had just gotten her second DUI and was in a sober house. Mothering four children, she had eventually stopped working and let her CRNA certification lapse. This was an agreed strategy between her and her husband, she said, until her steady drinking became problematic. Her husband was devastated and frustrated, but divorce was not on the table yet. She told me this was her last chance. I was seeing myself two relapses ago and reminded that I was fucking up my last chance as we spoke. We caught up for a bit, and I lauded her for her strength. We traded numbers and I made an empty promise to meet up with her at a meeting again.

A few weeks later, I was in a sober house again and we saw each other at another meeting. She had the peace of early sobriety and at least the surface acceptance it gives you as she sat knitting during the meeting. I gave a mumbled explanation regarding my latest fall, and now it was her turn to tell me, "It's okay." We did not speak again until the summer of 2020. She called me one day and we caught up on our sob stories. After a third DUI, she was now going through divorce and living in her own apartment. She asked if I wanted to meet up for dinner. By then it was becoming apparent that C.C. had put herself back on the market. I was still in love with her, but the only thing more pathetic than a bachelor is a celibate one. "Get busy livin' or get busy dyin'."

She cooked a beautiful dinner at her place, which was way nicer than mine, and we just talked for a while. C.C. and I were together for twenty-five years. I forgot what it was like to discover someone new; I never thought I would need to again. Anna and I knew each other, but we were not the people who toiled through anesthesia school together. It just felt nice to have a connection like that again. She had a sizable settlement from her divorce and talked about her plans for going back to school to become a counselor. My heart broke for her as she teared up talking about her children, whom she had not seen in months. Her custody agreement mandated that she had to show lasting sobriety to be back in their lives. It got intimate quick; we just both needed that release. For a little more than a month, once a week, that was our regular thing—dinner and companionship, with some TV and talk thrown in for good measure. She said she did not want any more from me, and I was content with our relationship as it was.

One night, I knocked on her door. She was usually quick to answer with her pretty smile; we would kiss, embrace for a few moments, and just enjoy being with each other. That night, I knocked again, then a third time. I texted her to see if maybe she had dozed off. She threw the door open, her smile wide and wild, the momentum from the door almost taking her off her feet before I caught her. The way your brain tries to complete the pandemic profile of someone you just met, filling in the puzzle under the mask, I was using what I had to solve what was happening to Anna. When she fell into my arms, her smell took the fun out of the game; she was drunk. She admitted as much, then started to rationalize it, saying she only wanted one bottle of wine, but the liquor store had a BOGO sale, and she could not pass that up and then she was only going to drink one but it was so good and then they were both gone and then she—

"Stop," I said.

I was breathing heavy and resisted the urge to turn around and run. She pulled me into the kitchen, said that dinner was ready, and she blew into her interlock, the breathalyzer linked to the starter in her car, and it turned red so it wouldn't start but it's probably fine and her sponsor told her to tell me not to come over—

"Anna, stop." There were empty wine bottles and a bottle of gin littering the countertop. I felt like I was walking into traffic. "Your children," was all I could say. She started to tear up. She kept telling me she made a mistake, but it was going to be okay. Watching her face undulating through emotion, from joy to doubt to fear to terror as the buzz wore off, was like looking in a mirror; I knew how it felt from the other side. She smiled again and got up, pulling me in to her room. I told her I could not be there. Alcohol erasing all inhibition, she erupted, saying she wanted me to be a part of her life and we belonged together, and she was falling in love with me. There was a part of me that wanted to say "fuck it," and jump on the oblivion train with her, but I knew there would be no stop. So, I stopped her, I told her I was sorry, and I would always be there for her, but I could not be with her right now. I called her sponsor and told Anna I would call her the next day. And then I got the fuck out.

The next day, Anna had the familiar remorse and regret in her voice as she picked up the pieces. She wanted to see me. I told her I was conflicted and scared. I could not put what I had in jeopardy, and I needed stability in my life. I told her to call me if she needed to talk but I could not be with her until she was in a better place. Two days later, she texted me and said she was better and wanted me to come over. I told her it was not the right time. What I did not tell her was that it would never be the right time. I felt I was barely holding on to my own sobriety—there was no way we could stay sober together.

Two days later, Anna died from a drug overdose.

I am not a special butterfly. Just as I did not have the power to keep Bo sober, I did not have the power to drive a woman to suicide. But you could not tell me that when I first learned she was dead. I found out a few weeks later through a Facebook message from another colleague from school. I felt sick. My head was spinning. She did not even use drugs. Who found her? What did her kids say? Oh, God, her kids. *She is dead because of me.* It took weeks and the fine people in my counseling group and twelve-step meetings to help me accept it was not my fault. I know I did not kill her, but to this day, I cannot totally exonerate myself. There is a fine line between being selfish for your own safety and self-centered because you just do not care. C.C. taught me that. She divorced me in rehab when I had no home and no future, not out of spite, but to save her life and the lives of my children. She made the hard choices and got through it.

It took a long time for me to accept that I walked away from Anna because I didn't want to lose all I had fought to gain. It is easier to save someone else than to save ourselves; but we can lose ourselves in the process. For years I had taken the "easier, softer way," tiptoeing around the path to sobriety I never wanted but needed to walk. The brutal truth of me was too hard to get through so I avoided it. I would not let Anna's sacrifice be a waste of a beautiful person. I hold her lesson in my heart to this day so that I will not repeat it. I am alive today because I go through my life. I face the hard truth in the mirror every day, try to be a living amends to those I have harmed, and do what I must to remain sober. There is no going back.

The Only Way Out Is Through

WE ALL FACE two options when dealing with life—go around or go through. We gain nothing worthwhile in life by going around it. We go through school for a better education. We—well, many of us—go through childbirth to make miracles happen. We go through counseling to gain a new perspective on our lives. We can go around, following that brambled, convoluted path, and get stuck in a job we do not want or with a person that kills us softly, numbing ourselves to the pain, or we can TEAR (Talk, Empower, Abandon, Recover) through.

Talk—Forget drugs, alcohol, or anything else that takes you out of yourself. There is nothing more effective than sharing your feelings with someone you trust. Out in the open, our pain and shame lose their power.

Empower yourself. Believe you can make the changes you must and take action.

Abandon your old ways of thinking and behavior. Often, no one can ruin our lives faster than we can. Consider your contribution to your conundrum and make the necessary change. Don't ruin your life; run it.

Recover—Realize your crisis is not your life. Give yourself the time to get through it to a better place.

I cannot, in good conscience, recommend anyone follow my path, but I believe I would not be the man I am today, which is arguably my best self, without going through all I have. Your best life is out there, but you must get to it. Do not be a slave to your circumstances, regardless if they are self-imposed or out of your control. Go through the cannon smoke and bear those scars proudly. There is always a way out. Rip and TEAR till you find it.

14

GRIEF INTERRUPTED

Fuck Facebook. Now, before I get thrown in a Meta-gulag where I am sentenced to play *FarmVille* for life, let me explain. I was never a big social media guy. Sure, I created an account back when everyone else did, mostly to stay in touch with my brother who had just joined the Navy and throw up pics of Cleo and Adam. Beyond watching with the morbid fascination of rubbernecking a car wreck as the world became obsessed with posting everything from what they ate for breakfast to career-ending photos, the social network was an inane waste of time to me. C.C. posted more than I, and just as she wasted no spoken word or emotion, all she put out into the digital ether was from her heart. From pictures of us as a happy family on vacations, to an annual throwback photo of our wedding day on our anniversary, with a little blurb counting each time how many years ago she married her "best friend," to serene pictures from the deck of our mountain vacation home with the comment, "Feeling blessed," in contrast to the 99.9 percent of nonsense that permeated the social landscape, everything she posted dripped with genuine joy.

It gave me joy to know how devoted she stayed to me, even after all I put her through in our decades together. I needed those encouraging words; the heart and kissy emojis gave them even more impact. My Facebook posts have a historically negative correlation with my misery. After the big fall and our divorce, I did not post anything for years, save a pic of my one-year sobriety coin. I avoided my feed as well; seeing others live their happy lives when I had made such a mess of mine just made me feel worse. C.C. and I barely talked about us. I could not help but click on her posts as she came back to the world, reading her poetic soliloquies about the light reentering her life. There was always a serene vista of the lake or vacation spot where she took the kids with commentary about healing and growth. I was grateful I did not destroy her spirit; I did not have that power, and she never would have let me if I did. But I felt left behind as she worked to recover from the sickness I gave her, already jealous of the life she was living without me.

I was tagged in posts, however. One I was proud of; it was a short film I had made about my Avenues experience and posted it on their Facebook page. The other, I believe, was partly responsible for C.C. pulling the trigger on our divorce. One of the purposes of rehab is to back you off the ledge; sometimes that involves infusing levity into what can be an intense and harrowing few months. It was Halloween and a few of us dressed up. We attended our sessions for the day in costume and got together for a group photo outside. Totally harmless. I got tagged in it and apparently C.C. had not yet unfriended me. Out of context, it looked bad; she was barely holding it together as a single mom, and I am dressed up like Freddy Krueger with my arm around a slutty Harley Quinn. Nothing is trivial. To be clear, it was my pathological lying and refusal to stay sober that got me divorced, but that pic was one of the last twists of my knife, which she finally pulled out. She accepted C.C. and Sloane were over; it would take me much longer to do the same.

We will get back to the social dilemma but allow me to catch you up one last time. After Anna's death, I gave up on relationships for a while. I focused on myself, my children, and work, not always in that order. I was clean just over two years now. It was not the longest period of sobriety I have had, but it was the longest I had stayed invested in my recovery; besides Cleo and Adam, it was the only meaning I had in my life. I looked forward to my meetings and support groups each week; in the past, I was just there to get signatures I had to provide the Board to show my continued compliance with the program. Even then, when I was pretending at being a person, I never left a meeting without a change in my perspective, however small. Just the catharsis of unloading your soul among the most impartial crowd you will encounter is worth the buck you toss in the collection basket, let alone hearing others' stories. I have a legion of family and friends and fans that would halt their lives to hear what I have to say, but I was never able to empty my tank as completely as I could in one of the rooms.

I had spent the last few years trying not to feel, disconnecting all those unwanted emotions, sadness, regret, love, and all their annoying cousins. I even paid out of pocket for another antidepressant, the emotional equivalent of a chemical coma. But I could not keep them offline forever. Once you start feeling again, like Covid finally releasing your taste and smell, they come out in spurts, layered with feelings you forgot you had—it is hard to turn off, all that vulnerability simmering just under the surface. It bubbles over when you do not expect it. I realized I was trying to bury that vulnerability all my life in drugs, alcohol, exercise, and anything else that either numbed it or caused me pain on my own terms. Chemical peace was not the answer. What I needed was an emotional ablation.

In medicine, cardiac ablations are performed on patients with potentially life-threatening arrythmias, or irregular heart rhythms. Like any physical or emotional blight on the heart, these can be held at bay with drugs for a while, but the best odds of ridding the body of it is with an ablation, the kind St. Peg drove herself to get decades ago. During the procedure, catheters are inserted into the groin and snaked up through the body's vasculature to the heart. The arrhythmia is induced through electrical signals, essentially dragging it out of hiding. Once in plain sight, the aberrant impulse causing havoc in the heart is literally burned away. A room full of sobriety surgeons can provide the same service for your soul for only a buck if you are so inclined. You do not even need a crowd, just one other who gets it. I rip the shame and fear and regret and resentment from within and toss it on the floor, where it writhes and wriggles and dies in the fire of solidarity.

These men and women, these MOTHS, have seen it all before. They just nod and let me keep dumping till it is done and then I join the crowd and help someone else do the same. Try it. And if you cannot find an appropriate room or someone you trust with your pain, then scream. Fill your lungs, bear down, and let out a fucking lion's call, a war cry. Do it again. Harder this time. Scream until your thought aches and your voice sounds like crushed glass. Scream until tears stream down your face. Scream until you sob like a baby. Scream until you can't breathe. Scream like it is the last sound you will ever make. Burn it out. Now breathe. In and out until you do it without shuddering. Wipe your nose, wipe your eyes, and do your day.

I did that almost every day for a few months; I still do sometimes. Regardless of the pain we cause, we still need to get rid of our own. Remember, pain is energy, and like all energy we pass it along to each other; we give it away only to receive it again one day. I transferred so much of it to C.C., she finally had to give it back. But even its ablation is not permanent. There must be a deeper change within us to bring true peace.

You do not have to be an addict to know the Serenity Prayer:

· · ·

"GOD (OR DEITY/HIGHER *power of choice), grant me the serenity to accept the things I cannot change, the courage to change the things I can, and the wisdom to know the difference.*"

IT IS AN EVERY-PRAYER FOR EVERYONE, regardless of faith, or lack thereof, useful in times of crisis and peace. As we recite it, we ask for some fine virtues like serenity, courage, and wisdom, but the most critical request is to *accept.* I admitted I was all that was wrong with my life, that I was the villain, but I never accepted I could be more. I was supposed to be the hero; I was supposed to be the shining example of how to live right. My inability to accept myself, good and bad, was the root of all my pain. While C.C. was moving on, I was trying to restart the cycle that always ended the same way before looping around again. This was apparent when I would visit Cleo and Adam in my old home. Since the day I left four years ago, it has always been painful to return; it is a constant reminder of what I gave up for one more run.

The first few months after our divorce was official were the worst. Instead of casually walking in through the garage door, I knocked on the red door of our dream suburban colonial; only delivery drivers and political lobbyists knocked on that door. C.C. had lost what little faith she had left in me, so all my visits were supervised. For a time, this place, which used to be my home, was the only evidence I had that time was moving forward, albeit without me. Once or twice a week, I would knock. At first it was always C.C. that would answer. When you have been with someone for a quarter century, it is common for communication to use less words and more body. Human beings can express about six basic emotions, universally recognized, and interpreted through specific facial expressions. I mentioned before that C.C. wore her heart on her sleeve, or more appropriately for her, on her cheeks. She had answered the door for me before when she would hear me fumbling with the keys or I forgot them. Her beautiful face was always smiling, her almond eyes narrowing, her full lips stretching into the shadows of her high cheekbones. She was happy. Other times, the shadows stayed long, her lips pursed together, her eyes neutral and beaming right through me. She was annoyed or angry.

Then, in the time after the extraordinary betrayal, there was always a slight wrinkle in her nose. Disgust. It is always painful being there, but my heart lies with my children now and that is where they are. Both teenagers now, it feels like they tolerate me, but that is to be expected. They were fifteen and eleven when I left, and my heart broke all over again. I could never imagine being here until I was. I lost my father, at least the man I knew and loved, at thirteen. Did my kids lose theirs? Still, when I saw them, it felt, if even for a few moments, that all the bad was wiped away. With each visit, though, the house changed. Our rustic décor replaced with framed Hallmark card platitudes from the Target Magnolia display. Warm, cherrywood cabinets and dark granite countertops whitewashed into a sterile farmhouse chic, wiping away any trace of color, any trace of me. To her, it was a canvas for her full pop-country transition. To me, it was erasure.

By then, I was on my apology tour, part of the ninth step in AA, where we make amends to those we have harmed. It was an essential and humbling experience to admit my faults and pledge my living amends to them, to spend my life making up for all the trouble I caused them. I called up old employers, even the nurse who blew the whistle on me in my last anesthesia job. I talked to my mom and my siblings and, most importantly, Cleo and Adam. They have been on my roller coaster as long as they have been alive, and I needed them to know I took responsibility for all that has happened to our family. I told them my father died from this disease and I would not do that to them. I told them there is nothing more important than being honest and that they can talk to me about anything, especially if they feel they are on a dark path. Echoing the promise I made to Cleo when she was minutes old, I told them I would always be there for them, for as long as I live. They both looked at me with a teenager's mute discomfort when real talk is involved, but they listened. I thanked them and told them I loved them. I prepared an amends for C.C., but she told me she did not want it, nor did she want me to make an amends to her parents.

I made a desperation amends to her shortly before our divorce and well before I had earned the right to. She knew it was bullshit and like the boy who cried wolf. Even after I had worked with my AA sponsor to make a proper amends, she said she no longer cared about what I was doing for my recovery. She had heard it all before and she always caught the shrapnel of my choices; it was about her now and our children and rightly so. For someone like me, who spent more time in my head than reality, she was my tether to the world, to sanity, to practicality. I could go as far down the rabbit hole as she would allow, always tugging to be back when I got too deep. I loved her for that. I needed her for that. As you can expect, she wanted to be more than just my tether. I cannot blame her, and I should not resent her, but it still bubbles up out of the mire now and again, usually when our banter becomes almost like we are still a couple again, then she interjects with cold practicality that casual cruelty to remind me that it is over. It has been over; I am just still in denial. But rather than accept she was healing in her own way, reaching the final stage of grief over a love she tried so hard to keep alive, I dusted off my resentments and thought, *If she has moved on, I have too.* But that was just my indifference identifying as acceptance. I did what I must to stay clean and in my children's lives; I kept ablating my pain in my counseling groups and meetings and stayed compliant with the Board's monitoring program, which included random urine screening for drugs and alcohol.

How have I gotten this far into my little tale of tragedy and triumph without touching on the singular experience of someone watching you pee in a cup? On average of twice per month, I was called in to an approved testing site to submit a urine specimen; sometimes they would draw blood, but it was almost always urine. As I am a three-time recipient of a "stayed suspension in favor of probation," otherwise known as "high risk," all my screens were observed. A male staff member was required to watch my pee-porn, usually some mouth breather that stood in the corner while I tried to overcome stage fright. During the first year of Covid, though, staff was tight in approved urgent care clinics and testing sites so, when no bros were available, women were tapped to watch me drain my tap. One female staff member tasked with watching my willy to detect any deception was quite fastidious in her duty. She got eye-level with my third eye, her face six inches away from my six inches; I mean seven inches. She watched and waited, and I used every trick in the book for curing my paruresis under pressure; I played word scramble with the "American Standard" scrawled on the porcelain, held my breath so the resulting buildup of carbon dioxide dumping into my circulation would relax my bladder, and anything else that would just let me pee. Finally, the floodgates opened, and I heard the hollow pittle of piss hitting plastic.

"There we go!" she cheered with a mother's exuberance over her toddler going potty for the first time. I stopped feeling humiliated a long time ago. Every time I stood there, pleading with my bladder to stop being so shy, I would say to myself, "I earned this." Not deserved, earned. Three tours through the Board monitoring program and more than twelve years of pissing in cups, and I earned all of it. I say *earn* because *deserve* carries a negative connotation for me, stemming back to elementary school, with nuns jabbing me in the chest with their bony fingers, cawing, "You got what you deserve," when they would catch me screwing around in class, or my mom echoing their chastising while punishing me after she caught me lying about something. *Deserve* is a very subjective word. Misbehaving kids deserve punishment; criminals deserve prison; C.C. said she deserved better than me.

To me, *deserve* sounds too much like just deserts, of which I have received more than enough. I never believed I deserved anything, least of all anything good, even when I was told I did. To me, *deserve* always carried an air of being an entitled shit, which I never accepted I was. If you believe Bible-thumping Elvin from Calvary Chapel, "If we got what we deserve, we'd all be dead."

So, when I sat in an interview for yet another incredible opportunity to again reprise my role as a nurse anesthetist, I kept thinking, *I do not deserve this.* During the six months of administrative hoops I had to jump through, interrogative interviews with the credentialing staff and the chief of anesthesia singing the praises of a man he hardly knew but believed in anyway to the hospital board, that refrain kept playing in my head: *I do not deserve this.* Even after the Board of Nursing gave me the go-ahead to return to anesthesia again, my professional association granting my recertification after disclosure of my crimes and being out of practice for nearly three years, I still did not believe I deserved something good. As I started my first day, back at the head of the bed, after three years of the hope, horror, and healing of sobriety, I did not know if anyone deserves a fourth chance, but I sure as hell earned it. I felt less like a feral William Wallace, howling at the sky after his first victory against the English, and more like Andy Dufresne crawling through five football fields of shit, but my head was up just the same. If you stay clean from whatever ails you, life will get better; I promise.

Of course, having a lucrative job I respected again was not the endgame, but my redemption in the profession was important to me. People I trust asked me if this was the best place for me; I literally draw up and administer fentanyl, the drug that nearly killed me and symbolized my reckless ruin of my family, every day. One thing I can say with rigorous honesty is that, after twenty years, I finally know my enemy. Monitoring through drug screens was always a deterrent for me. When none of the lessons of a century of AA empirical evidence convinced me how to stay sober, fear of getting caught again always did. When the institution where I now work insisted I enter a monitoring contract for the duration of my employment there, I just said, "Where do I sign?" There is more to it than that, of course; I still make a daily decision to stay clean and I know I will always be at risk. But I got people, a host of angels, in my corner, some old, some new, who keep me honest, as I do for them.

Though I downsized my roller coaster from the steep hills and looping thrills on tubular steel to the palm-sweating jank and sharp sways of wood, I was still on it, and what goes up must come down. After the first week at my new job, accepting I was where I belong and finding much-needed peace of mind, C.C. told me she had been seeing someone for six months. I suspected; when I would visit the kids, she would pass me on the way out smelling and looking pretty with a bottle of wine and two glasses. During one of our conversations months after my failed attempt at another amends, almost out of the blue she said, "I forgive you," which, in retrospect, as my absolution coincided with her getting back on the market, sounded more like, "I'm fucking someone else." C.C. never made decisions lightly; if she had been with this dude that long, it was serious. I had no right to be upset. I had been with someone else, and she had done the work to get through her grief; she survived me and earned the right to get what she wanted.

My grief finally called in its debt. It had been nearly three years since my extraordinary betrayal, but it felt like three days—the pain raw and throbbing as I played Kubler-Ross whack-a-mole with all five stages popping up at random. The next few days I could barely sleep, tears coming at random, my heart going bang, bang, bang, tripping over itself, skipping beats; I feared I would need an actual ablation. I talked about it with my brothers, my recovery posse, and my counselor; they all gave me the same advice: accept it and move on. I knew I had no right to the anger and resentment that bubbled back up, but I let it come anyway, realizing my peace in recovery was gossamer thin; all it took was some harsh truth or a Facebook pic to pull it apart. The rickety ride continued.

The initial shock, then my mind tried to compensate, flooding my bloodstream with serotonin, already segmenting the memory of it, breaking it into chunks so I could not feel the full weight of it. Then I started to imagine I could have a life after this. Up. Then she broke the news that she'd been seeing someone who knew who he was, was successful, owned four properties, and she really liked him. Just a month ago, I gushed on my defunct wedding anniversary how I would always love her. I am still pissed she let me go on like that; she had already been with another guy for six months. Down. Then I created a Tinder account for reactionary sex and accidentally met someone who was passionate and knew what she wanted and who made me feel like the center of the universe. I never believed I would find another that would accept me as C.C. had. Up. Then I dropped off my kids on Christmas Day and saw the boyfriend cuddling up to her in my old living room where we lived and laughed and made love, and I am supposed to be all mea fucking culpa? Down. I moved into a new place that Nicole, my new love, helped me decorate to make my own. I was candid with her about my unresolved feelings for C.C. and our long life together. Her acceptance of my unacceptance was remarkable. She saw me still on my ride, but convinced me to slow down and admire the scenery. Up. Then I clicked on a fucking Facebook post that felt like getting my finger caught in one of those neck-snapping mouse-traps that I knew I should not have. There was the email notif-ication, "C.C. Ellis posted a new photo." I knew the happy couple was away that weekend because I stayed at her house with my kids. They were the only reason I would I even drive down my old block, let alone stay and sleep under the same roof, because they were the only reason I would get uncomfortable, because she knew I would do anything to be with them. *Don't open it, don't you fucking open it.* I opened it. And there they were. After eighteen months, she was stepping out with her new love. It was not her smile while she leaned on him, her long hair tangled in his, which looked brighter than any she had sitting next to me, that hurt like a kick to the groin. It was what she said underneath it: "The man who brought my joy back." Down and coast to the end. We hope you enjoyed your ride—please collect your belongings and watch your step on the way out.

Yep, ultimately it was the metaverse that helped give me closure on my relationship with C.C.—that and some help from my family. The thorn that remained lodged in my side, the truth over which I could not stop sobbing like a butt-hurt tween, is that while I just needed her, she just needed someone. I was never the guy who dreamed he would be married with kids one day; our marriage and family were extensions of an uncommon love that I never expected to find. When it was all over, it felt like after twenty-five years, I was replaced by another piece of meat just like that, except it is not like that. I did not know how low she got in the first year. I saw glimpses, her gaunt cheeks, her occasional lash-out when I brought us up. When she wrote her final letter to me, it was a well-constructed goodbye—no fluff, no wasted words, infused with the hard research. She was brilliant at distilling feeling into fact and presenting it with no ambivalence. As I said, you always know where you stand with her. And that was apparently the PG-13 version. She said she would never tell me the depths she sank to, that it would push me over the edge, that it would shatter the fragile peace I have made with myself.

I remember every accusation and harsh truth C.C. gave me like a prayer I learned as a kid. But as C.C. said to me, I could not see the circle of love I had, all the love she gave me and proclaimed with her words to me and on a social network and to her friends and family. I only remember the bad. My damaged mind or my choice? She is just being who she is now with someone else, and I just could not handle it. I could not accept it.

I kept asking myself, "How? How can I ever get through this?" Accepting we were done meant that I accept that I was the only thing wrong with us. Accepting I had to move on felt like I was leaving behind the best parts of myself, the parts she gave me. But I must. When life hits us with both fists, if we want to live in any semblance of peace, we must accept what we cannot change. If not, all the bad stuff seeps in, the resentments, the anger, the shame. It slow walks us. It will catch us eventually and never when we are ready for it. Even if it is not a full relapse on a substance or person or thing, it is the consequences. They will haunt us forever. Then it is up to us what we do next. We must accept who and what we are, good and bad. Then accept that we can be more.

All told, it took a year for me to work through my delayed grief, starting with C.C. throwing off the last of my emotional anchors to her, sailing away with another, and my coming to grips with throwing away a beautiful life. There is no template for this process. Addiction, or any way of living that relegates us to a passenger in our own life, opens a path that never covers over. I wake up some days and still find myself there, tripping over knotted memories—it is no longer paved with a false diamond-crusted shimmer of new macadam. Some days, I wallow in the same rotten headspace, thorns of regret pulling at my legs, traversing a life I don't recognize, adjusting to another "new normal," changing my identity from "we" to "me."

I spent years trying not to live. And just as needles cascade through frostbitten fingers now thawing by a fire, the ache of life throbs as I reach back out to friends, seek love again, or at least what I understand as love, pay bills, and evaluate my future now that it seems I will live a while longer, albeit with more honesty and humility. At first, my only measure of my zest for life was my willingness to engage in preventive healthcare. Dermatologists, orthodontists, gastroenterologists are the luxuries of the living. In stroke patients, you notice an abandonment of the side of the body affected by the stroke; even your own body is divided into cliques. If one side can no longer keep up, the rest of you leaves it behind. When you do not care if you live or die, you sure as hell do not care about pearly whites or the tip-of-the-iceberg devastation of colon polyps. The day I tried to live again, I dusted off my insurance cards. I was not looking for anything as lofty as joy just yet. I was just trying to look at myself in the mirror again. Time does its thing, smoothing out the jagged edges of regret, and I started to feel worthy of what had been returned to me, my relationship with my children, my career, self-worth, and came closer to closure over what was taken away.

C.C. was happy in a life now in which I could never be a part. It had been a long time since C.C. and Sloane made more than two hundred of our friends and family sway with love and awe during our final dance at our wedding. We made a good yin and yang; her sky car and my wild ride were opposites that made a beautiful whole. But I do not know if the puzzle of us ever fit together properly, or maybe I just was incapable of being in a loving relationship, as she said, and sabotaged it from the start. Which brings us back to that timeless question with no answer: "Why?" Why did I pop those pills all those years ago? Why did I go from a man capable of living and loving to a slave shackled by all my worst defects of character?

Years of counseling and a genuine desire to pick out the culprit on a proverbial lineup suggested by loved ones and paid ones have turned the inside of my head into a conspiracy theorist's bedroom, neurons stretched across a mindscape of events and suppressed trauma like red yarn, trying to connect the dots, trying to map out why I implode my life every few years. That room has been long abandoned; I just don't have the time left to figure it out. I gave up on that part of myself long ago. Now I just live, with help from others like me, with the support of family and friends who just can't quit me, like my mom and her youngest sister, my aunt Denise. They are sitting with me in my old backyard as we celebrate the high school graduation of my extraordinary Cleo, the self-styled One Who Creates. Besides the three of us, C.C.'s entire extended family is in attendance, including her new love. I was not looking forward to going; I had not interacted with most of her family, people I was once very close to, in any meaningful way the last few years. But this was about Cleo, so I swallowed my shame and ego and walked up the driveway with cupcakes.

I figured I would stay for an hour just to make good on my promise to Cleo that I would always be there, be cordial, and drive home in tears. Four hours later, I was still laughing with former in-laws and old neighbors and enjoying their company. C.C.'s family seemed genuinely happy to see me alive and well and I relished the chance to catch up and wax nostalgic. And then there was C.C.. She has said to me countless times, all she wanted was for me to be happy. She spent most of our time together trying to ensure that, often at the expense of her own. And seeing her that day, her smile as beaming and vibrant as the first time I saw her, getting out from under the addiction and personality disorders and whatever the fuck else held me back from being a whole and healthy person, I realized I just wanted her to be happy, too, even if it is not with me. Seeing those static Facebook images broke my heart, but seeing her in motion, flowing through her life, happy and whole, finally gave me the acceptance I needed. Today, I am happy she is happy and living the life she deserves and has more than earned.

As for me, some days I am engaged with the world, smiling and greeting perfect strangers, working hard, and watching my children grow into remarkable adults. I remain invested in my sobriety, body, and mind, remaining patient as people ablate their own sickness. Other days, I just want to be the guy in the "Bittersweet Symphony" video. It is a process, but I am learning to trust it. Life goes on, as it always does, and for the first time in a long time, I am going along with it.

ACCEPTANCE IS THE ANSWER

I could save you my soliloquy and recommend reading *Acceptance Was the Answer* in the in the Big Book, but then you would miss out on my penultimate cringy acronym (you should still read it). (Wilson, Acceptance Was the Answer, 2001) Acceptance is the solution to most of our problems. I spent years hating the world because my view of it was at odds with what was "normal." Even when I admitted responsibility for my actions and owned the consequences, I struggled to understand that vital request in the Serenity Prayer to "accept the things I cannot change and the courage to change the things I can." I always asked myself "How." How can we accept the loss of a relationship that defined us or the loss of someone close? How do we accept that we may be the only thing wrong in our lives? How do we accept our banger of a Facebook post only got five likes? Don't ask yourself how. Tell yourself HOW (Honest, Open-minded, Willing). (Wilson, 2001) I am adopting this straight from the Big Book, but it is worth the plagiarism.

Be **Honest** with yourself and others about your feelings. There is no how you should feel, only how you do feel. Do not hold it in. I was the root of all my problems, but it was my incapacity for honesty that was at the root of me.

Be **Open-minded** about ways to move forward. I tried a bunch: rehabs, psychotherapy, couples counseling, priests, street preachers, twelve-step meetings, horse therapy and medication, legal and illegal. All, except for my abuse of drugs and alcohol, were potentially life changing, had I been open to the change, but I was still playing God. Find what works for you and stay with it.

Have the **Willingness** to accept and to change. We cannot accomplish anything without the will to do so first. It takes work to get better. It can be unbearable. And there is no guarantee what is on the other side. But I can guarantee that it is better than where you are now. Just as the demons are patient, so is peace. It will settle within you if you accept it.

PLAN B

"If you want to hear God laugh, make plans." That was a mantra I first heard uttered by my Irish Catholic elders when I was young, and through recovery-based literature, twelve-step meetings, and my own experience, I have been painfully reacquainted with the aphorism. Whether you believe a God laughs at you or even exists, few of us are strangers to our grand designs going awry. But still, we design them. We all want to achieve things, from perhaps something as grand as retiring on our own island to something as ostensibly trivial as getting through a day without once thinking about all the things we fucked up. Any goal needs a plan, a way to get from where you are to where you want to be. We work to make money to go to school to get a job making more money to afford more school to get a better job making even more money. We plan weddings, we plan parties, vacations, weddings, families, and retirement. We plan to get in and out of relationships. We plan futures. Some of those plans come to fruition even though they may not look the way we envisioned. Like a commissioned work of art, for instance, it is what we asked for, but the line work and color hues are slightly off what we envisioned. We are not where we thought we would be or with the ones we thought we wanted to be.

I do not have a fastidiously researched and reliable census, but based on my own empirical evidence, I believe most people are not yet living the life they intended. C.C. had plans; they were plans I wanted to be a part of, to enjoy with her, but she designed them and painted a vision for me, a beautiful palette of us in another place, like the mountains of Colorado, the beaches of Hawaii, or any one of the many places she took us to fall back in love. She had real plans, a retirement together for which we would be financially and emotionally ready. At least, I thought I would be ready when the time came. This future always lingered on the horizon, and I genuinely wanted it.

But I had a plan too.

My plan was to keep chasing those first few euphoric trips, with opiates, alcohol, and any other substance that made me feel like anything but me. I twisted in the insanity of trying to achieve the endgame of all addicts—to indulge in my vices with impunity. Every time I would get clean and buy back the trust, love, and respect I sold for another run, I would start laying out a strategy for the next one; except "this time," I would do it right. It might take years, but I kept nurturing the insane hope that I could find my chemical peace again without getting found out. This was not a good plan, and the shred of rationality I kept on hand told me it would never work, but I kept trying, analyzing my mistakes of the past and looking forward to a future where I could coexist in harmony with my addiction, always refusing to live in the beauty of what is.

Not long ago, I was fulfilling my community service hours, working off the probation from my misdemeanors, at a local nonprofit donation center. What I imagined would be standard volunteer work became something far more meaningful. During my fifty hours there, broken up into five- or six-hour days, I added some new angels to my pantheon. Eva, a top-hat sporting artist and curator of the pre-owned presents dropped off every day, offered me the volunteer position. The egress of some serious ink through her joggers and the sleeves and high neckline of her blouse betrayed her demure beauty; it was comforting to be in the company of someone else with a past hidden in plain sight.

I accepted donations and lifted heavy things, most often with David, a hardworking college kid who could be Adam in five years, and my newest would-be father figure, Bill, the Everyman of the store whose round, smiling face was proof of a life well lived. All donations were distilled into six categories. There were typical recycled relics like clothes, toys, and DVDs; "domestics" were things like blankets and bedding; the "bric and brac" bin was a collection of everything else, from kitchenware to hideous handcrafted sculptures. Then there were lots of books. For someone like me, haunted by a past I was trying to forget, while paging through old books to assess their value, I was enamored by notes scrawled in the margins in some and dedications to loved ones in others. Most of the notes seemed to hold secrets, their meaning and context known only to scribe and recipient. These shards of stories within stories, imbuing their memories with a fragile immortality, filled me with a nostalgia that made it hard for me to forget my own memories. I stopped paging through them, resigned to literally judge the books by their cover. Then, one day, organizing a crate of newly delivered used books, I saw it.

Holy shit.

Wedged between Clive Cussler and Patricia Cornwell was a Dr. Seuss book I had not seen since it had scared the living shit out of me as a boy. After staring at it, motionless, for a few moments I picked it up by one of its edges the way you might handle a suspected murder weapon. There was a different title on the cover from what I remembered. *What Was I Scared Of?* (Geisel, 2009) it called itself these days, like it had been in hiding for years under a different name. But as I turned through the splash pages of a disembodied pair of pants chasing a distinctive "Seuss Kid" through Seussian, fever dream landscapes, there was no question—this was the book formerly known as *The Pale Green Pants*, and to my young mind, it was terrifying. I mentioned a while back my dad was not one for reading bedtime stories, but when I was a boy, I begged him to read it to me. With the elemental fear of watching a giant spider spin its web, I watched my dad page through the book, holding onto his arm as he read through its signature rhyming, alliteration, and repetition. I never got far enough into it to see its climax of the boy being cornered by the horrifying, mute set of slacks and, spoiler, realizing they were the perfect fit for him. Smiling with relief, he slides them on and walks off into the surreal sunset.

Looking at it now, the color palette washed out and less vivid, the pale green pants now more mustard, the book itself even shrunk down to the size of a drugstore paperback you grab off the spinning caddy, the inspirational themes of perseverance, doing the hard work, and finding the courage to be yourself are more apparent; maybe those are what I was scared of. Those shuddering memories of a childhood horror story have been replaced by one—the sound of my dad's glorious laugh as he realized, with genuine surprise, the pants were the boy's all along. Of course, there was a dedication in the front: "Where you walk, so do I. Dad."

No bullshit.

Any "Anonymous" group is based on achieving a "life beyond our wildest dreams." (Wilson, 2001) This is a subjective concept, but *beyond* is the key word as it refers to an existence we could not imagine before; one beyond materialistic pursuits and grandeur, attainable only after we are at true peace with ourselves. For many, that life is just being sober; for others, it is finding new perspective or a new calling in life as a counselor, using their old life experience to guide others. For me, I used to think it was reconciling with my ex-wife and being back under the same roof as my family, vowing to be the husband and father they deserved only to inevitably ruin it again. I must live with the knowledge I was the only thing wrong with us. Broken from birth, trying to live like a real person, I was empty inside, filling myself with what I thought a man should be, laced with what I wanted to be. But today I live with it rather than running from it.

Like "Seuss Kid," I was just a kid running from myself for most of my life. I started to think maybe he had a good plan and decided to try this "new normal" on for size; even though it is a contingency to the impossible life of controlled addiction without accountability or consequence, it fits well enough. I spent so much time trying not to care, forcing my focus on just one day at a time, I did not know if I could start again. More than three years of sobriety and my love for Cleo and Adam were the only embers of a good life I kept stoked. From there, I fanned the flames slowly, reaching back out to friends and family, taking pride in my work as a nurse and further entrenching myself in my recovery community and doing what I can to help others like me.

I am moving on with someone else as well. I never thought I could be in another relationship again. I am not the shiny new car driven off the lot all those years ago. Now I am used, no warranty, take it or leave it, even though I do exude a strange kind of charm. I did not know if I could be a reliable partner or worthy of another's love. But we find what we need when we least expect it. Nicole is a woman who has struggled with her own demons and heart break, but she is vibrant and loving and has shown me there is life after death. Her love and support have been instrumental in helping me shake out this "rehash" can of mine and make sense of it, turning into something meaningful and useful.

One day I woke up and that subtle sadness that always started the day was no longer there. Time heals all, but some scars remain. Scars remind us of the pain of our past, like the ones I sustained on my mangled foot all those years ago on Main Street and the arrogance and recklessness they represent. They remind me of my dad who had more scars than I could count, sutured together like Frankenstein, but who kept on going, until he could not. He was only a few years older than I am now when he died. When I look in the mirror, which I am no longer ashamed to do, I see more of him in me now than ever. That used to feel like a curse. Today, his face on mine, not as a mask but as a tribute, is a reminder not to lose my way and to honor a life he never had but would have loved.

When I started to organize this memory dump, I needed a theme to glue it all together. Counselors, family, and friends kept using the word *resilience* regarding my refusal to die through years of struggling with addiction and myself, as my dad had. Resilience seemed an appropriate backdrop in which to frame my lessons, but not because I embodied it. Remember, I am the bad guy in this story. The resilience of the true heroes—the people who have been in my life as long as I have and those I have loved, lost, and bled with along the way, those who owed me nothing, yet kept me alive and helped me find reasons to stay that way—is what this story is about. It is this resilience I channeled to achieve a life I could not have imagined; one where I am the whole person I could not have been before.

I always came first, and I still do, but today I live for what I can give. The world is still on a collision course with itself, but I have some things to offer it, even if I do not always want to be a part of it; I am here for the people in it I care about. Today, I still have doubt. I still have fear. I still let the occasional resentment bubble up through the mire of the stagnant shit thinking I did for years. Sometimes I still feel for a ring that I discarded long ago, feeling the phantom pain of a great love. Sometimes the desire of that chemical peace still aches in me. But these shortcomings do not necessarily mean I am heading toward relapse; they mean I am still human.

Today, I still have the same people in my corner, the same

opportunities, the same fortune. The only difference is me. Probably the most vital truth I have gleaned from this cycle of self-damnation, exile, and redemption is that I could not have learned what I have without it. Nothing trumps plodding through the emotional mud of experience. Today, I am sober through attrition, but finally accepting that it is a better way of life for me is what has given me peace. There is no easier, softer way. Today, I tread the path I avoided for most of my life, through the ephemeral laughter and tears and joy and pain, snagging myself on the thorns of regret and clearing the way forward. Today I do not obsess over what I am supposed to be; I focus on who I am. Like Dad, no questions, just facts.

For a long time, I thought all my little deaths and resurrections were preparing me for some grand plan or purpose, always looking for a tomorrow I would never be satisfied with, ignoring today, which was right where I belonged. We do not have to be here for a reason—that is too much hype to live up to. We just have to be here, if we want to be. There is a solution if we do not, which I contemplated, and I am glad I chose to stick around. But if you want to be here, in this usually rote, sometimes shitty, but ever-changing life, be HERE (Humble, Earnest, Resilient, Empathetic).

Humble—Realize your life is a gift, not an entitlement.

Earnest—We are not our thoughts and words; we are our actions. Don't fake it, make it.

Resilient—What does not kill us makes us stronger. Nurture that strength and be your own example.

Empathetic—People will piss us off; understand we all struggle with ourselves in some way. In AA we say, "Hit them with a prayer, not a chair."

If you have read this far, I thank you for honoring my roller-coaster ride and I sincerely hope you have found something in these pages to give you perspective in your own life and how to navigate it better. There are many more lessons to learn, and the world will present them when you are ready; and even if you are not. You may disagree with some of mine, or all of them, and that is fine. Think about your own lessons you have cultivated and make your own acronyms to use as a guide. We continue to grow, and often we need to refresh them or toss them out and try again. Life is the ultimate lesson, and we will not learn it until we are through. Tell your own story. I would love to read it.

The only day we must do is today. The future will come in its own time; until then, come, all you MOTHS, HURT yourself, PLAN, be MEAN, TEAR through your life, never stop telling yourself HOW, and be HERE when it does. As for what was, we should not close the door on our past. If we forget where we came from, whether we are genetically fated, victims of circumstance, or maestros of our own mess, we are doomed to go back. I can never forget mine, but now, I can at least close the cover on it. Do not mourn what was or fear what is to come; celebrate what is. Keep learning, keep fighting, keep living, and know you are not alone.

BIBLIOGRAPHY

Burne, P. (1847). *The Teetotaler's Compainion; or a Plea for Temperance.* London: Arthur Hall and Co.

Chapman, G. (2015). *The 5 Love Languages: The Secret to Love that Lasts.* Chicago: Northfield Publishing.

Darabont, F. (Director). (1994). *The Shawshank Redemption* [Motion Picture].

Geisel, T. S. (2009). *What Was I Scared Of?* New York City: Random House Books for Young Readers.

Hari, J. (2015). *Chasing the Scream: The First and Last Days of the War on Drugs.* New York: Bloomsbury.

Hetfield, J., Ulrich, L., & Hammet, K. (1986). Welcome Home (Sanitarium) [Recorded by Metallica]. Copenhagen, Denmark.

Most, J., Pressman, E., & Hill, G. &. (Directors). (1994). *The Crow* [Motion Picture].

Palahniuk, C. (1996). *Fight Club.* New York: W. W. Norton.

Perry, j., Tyler, S., & Child, D. (1989). F.I.N.E. [Recorded by Aerosmith]. Vancouver, Canada.

Robbins, A. (2019, November 18).

Rock, C. (1996, June 1). *Chris Rock: Brirng the Pain.* (C. Rock, Performer) Takoma Theater, Washington, D. C., Washington, D. C., USA.

Russo, A., & Russo, J. (Directors). (2019). *Avengers: Endgame* [Motion Picture].

SEPIA. (2022). *Green Card.* Philadelphia: SEPIA Literature.

Tzu, S., & Cleary, T. (2005). *The Art of War.* Boston: Shambhala Publications, Inc.

Wilson, B. (2001). Acceptance Was the Answer. In B. Wilson, *The Big Book (Alcoholics Anonymous) (Fourth Edition)* (pp. 407-420). New York: Alcoholics Anonymous World Services.

Wilson, B. (2001). The Big Book (Alcoholics Anonymous) (Fourth Edition). In B. Wilson, *The Big Book (Alcoholics Anonymous) (Fourth Edition)* (p. 58). New York: Alcoholics Anonymous World Services.

Woititz, J. G. (1990). *Adult Children of Alcoholics.* Deerfield Beach: Health Communications Inc.

DEDICATION

To Mom - thank you for your love, both tender and tough, and your undying support. You have always been my inspiration for a life well-lived. I would not be here without you.

To my siblings, T.O., Vinny and Helene - you are the examples I strive to embody. Thank you for all you are.

To my children, Adam and Cleo: you are my world. Never stop dreaming, never stop growing, never stop.

To "The Gang" - You taught me everything in life worth knowing. Thank you for being one of my only constants in a life of uncertainty.

To my Stand-in Saviors — you are little miracles, all.

To my brother and sisters in recovery, those with whom I laughed and cried, fought and bled, won and lost, to those still in the trenches, those that clawed their way our and those that will never leave - you helped me become the man I am and I will always carry your selflessness and sacrifices in my heart.

To my coach, whip-cracker and the man that made this all possible, Ramy Vance - thank you for helping me negotiate the labyrinth of self-publishing, keeping me on track, and continually assuring me I could accomplish my dream.

To C.C. – thank you for the love we shared and the life we had. Thank you for greatest gifts I possess – our children. Most of what is good in me came from you. I wish you nothing but the best.

To my love, Nicole - thank you for making life worth living again.

Made in the USA
Middletown, DE
18 January 2023

22439011R00132